HOOKED RUGS OF THE DEEP SOUTH

JESSIE A. TURBAYNE

Schiffer Publishing Ltd

4880 Lower Valley Road • Atglen, PA 19310

CONTENTS

Library of Congress Control Number: 2011924876

Cover photo: Rug hooked by Dean Black of Alabama

Designed by John P. Cheek
Cover design by Bruce Waters

Type set in Minion Pro/Zurich BT

ISBN: 978-0-7643-3801-4
Printed in Hong Kong

Schiffer Books are available at special discounts for bulk purchases for sales promotions or premiums. Special editions, including personalized covers, corporate imprints, and excerpts can be created in large quantities for special needs. For more information contact the publisher:

Published by Schiffer Publishing Ltd.
4880 Lower Valley Road
Atglen, PA 19310
Phone: (610) 593-1777; Fax: (610) 593-2002
E-mail: Info@schifferbooks.com

For the largest selection of fine reference books on this and related subjects, please visit our website at
www.schifferbooks.com
We are always looking for people to write books on new and related subjects. If you have an idea for a book please contact us at the above address.

This book may be purchased from the publisher.
Include $5.00 for shipping.
Please try your bookstore first.
You may write for a free catalog.

In Europe, Schiffer books are distributed by
Bushwood Books
6 Marksbury Ave.
Kew Gardens
Surrey TW9 4JF England
Phone: 44 (0) 20 8392 8585; Fax: 44 (0) 20 8392 9876
E-mail: info@bushwoodbooks.co.uk
Website: www.bushwoodbooks.co.uk

ACKNOWLEDGMENTS

I wish to extend my sincere gratitude to those who contributed to the making of this book.

With great admiration and sincere gratitude to Pete Schiffer, who carries on the fine tradition of Schiffer Publishing, Ltd. Thank you.

A very special word of thanks to my editors Douglas Congdon-Martin and Jennifer Savage. I would also like to thank Nancy Schiffer and the wonderful staff that is Schiffer Publishing Ltd.

Heartfelt appreciation to:

Michael, after all these years and all these books… you're still the one.

Rob, Molly, and Max for bringing so much joy into my life.

Jamie, who decades ago put a holey old rug in my hands and has taught me about antiques and life ever since.

Judy Yasi, trusted friend, fellow rug hooker, and my "technical advisor." You have taught this author a thing or two about computers and done so with patience and compassion…and with more than a few laughs. Thanks to you… another book.

Annie A. Spring — you are my source of inspiration.

"Auntie Fran" — Francesca Rossi Lehman — who teaches me how to be Italian and is always there to listen.

Mary T. Sullivan — who teaches me how to be Irish and graciously shares her love of life.

Patricia Filosa — thanks for being such a good friend; one of the few that I can call at 6 a.m.

I am especially indebted to Lisanne Miller, Eric Sandberg, and Nancy Thompson. Without your encouragement and efforts this book would not exist.

And to all the rug hooking artists in The Deep South… thank you. I now know what true Southern hospitality is all about.

Kind acknowledgements to: Candace Ballard; Jane Bussom; Sheri Bennett; Pris Buttler; Caraway Rug School: Brianna Deasy; Colleen Deasy; Nancy Hackney; Wilma Hill; Shelley Hoffman; Donna Holdiness; Suzanne Holtkamp; Jacque Juvenal; Carrie Martin; Joan McClung; Marge Mello; Kim Nixon; Laurie Robinson; Judy Schweitzer, Annie A. Spring; C. Allan Turbayne; Justina Rae Two Eagle; Faith Williston; and Elaine Zimney.

And a special nod to: Dixie; Poppy; Little Jessie; Cookie Lee Jones; Leggins McMurphy; Sweetie Pie Lo Mein; Oscar; Tobias; Toolie; Yanni II and Oliver Edward and Jack Yasi. You make life a little sweeter for all of us.

DEDICATION & AUTHOR'S PREFACE

To Lisanne Miller, Eric Sandberg, and Nancy Thompson.

For 40 years I have been involved with hooked rugs; buying and selling, conservation, restoration, teaching the craft, lecturing, and writing books. After my first book was published in 1991(and actually sold and sold well) I had the secret desire to write more hooking books than Pearl McGown, the Grande Dame of rug hooking. The Martha Stewart of the craft from the 1940s into the 1970s, every modern day rug hooker knows Pearl's name. She was, and still is, a rug hooking icon. Pearl McGown had authored four books. By 2007 I had authored seven. Wish fulfilled... I had surpassed my goal. The rug hookers were happy. The antique dealers and collectors were happy. Schiffer Publishing was happy. And I was happy. Mission accomplished. And although I had thoroughly enjoyed the experience, I had written enough books on hooked rugs to make everyone happy...or so I thought.

A chance meeting with Lisanne Miller, New Jersey native turned rug hooking Down Mainer changed all that. A few years back we shared a roast beef sandwich and a spirited conversation at a rug hooking workshop in Massachusetts. Leaving the corporate world behind, the energetic Lisanne was, at the time of our meeting, living in the coastal town of York, Maine. She designed and sold rug hooking patterns and taught the craft to a group of enthusiastic students. Husband Ron, a native of Mississippi, and also retired from the corporate world, ran a successful auction business. Life was good... until those long, snow-bound Maine winters just got to be a bit too much to deal with. The lure of warm weather beckoned Ron back home to Mississippi and the Millers moved. Our friendship and mutual interest in hooked rugs continued though many miles and many states separated us.

Taking her love of antiques and rug hooking talents south to Mississippi, Lisanne opened "P is for Primitive" in historic Canton, the town where George Clooney filmed "Oh Brother – Where Art Thou?" The "P" sells antiques, collectibles, and specialty foods, and offers rug hooking lessons, patterns, and supplies. Phone calls to me on the progress of her shop and popularity of rug hooking in The Deep South were always met with enthusiasm and very frankly... surprise. Surprise not about success of the shop but about rug hooking in Mississippi. My business travels have taken me throughout the United States and Canada. The Deep South was never known for its hooked rugs...or so I thought.

Lisanne routinely sent me images of "fabulous" hooked rugs and told me stories of their gifted makers. And on a rather regular schedule she would gently remind me that rug hookers of The Deep South deserved to be recognized. When asked, "Is there enough material in The Deep South for me to do an entire book?" She replied, "Of course, there is plenty. What can I do to help?"

Hesitant to do another book and needing to put out some "feelers," I called trusted friends and fellow rug hooking artists Eric Sandberg and Nancy Thompson, both from Georgia, and sought out their opinions on this possible new project. "Is there enough material in The Deep South for me to do an entire book?" "Of course... there is plenty. What can we do to help?"

And help they did. Lisanne Miller, Eric Sandberg, and Nancy Thompson went to work and spread the word about this "new book Jessie was doing."

Lisanne hosted rug hooking gatherings and hook-ins. Securing the services of a professional photographer, she offered Mississippi hooking artists and those from neighboring states the opportunity to have their hooked art documented for this book.

Eric Sandberg contacted his long list of Southern hooking artists and urged them, in his most charming manner, to participate in this project. When he wasn't enlisting rug hookers by phone, he made personal visits to homes of those whose work "just had to be in Jessie's new book."

Nancy Thompson, in her true cheerleader fashion, organized large groups of Georgia rug hookers and made sure their rugs were photographed. She gathered the necessary paperwork and sent piles of forms to my studio in Massachusetts, working long hours to make sure everything was in proper order.

Hundreds of rug hookers, in true Southern style, graciously came forward – willing to share their stories and hooked handwork. And so I began my job of writing *Hooked Rugs of The Deep South*; an experience I have truly enjoyed.

Author's note: Sadly, Nancy Thompson passed away in July 2010 and was unable to see this book in print. The epitome of Southern grace and charm, she was a dear lady and a talented rug hooking artist. Many will miss Nancy, including myself.

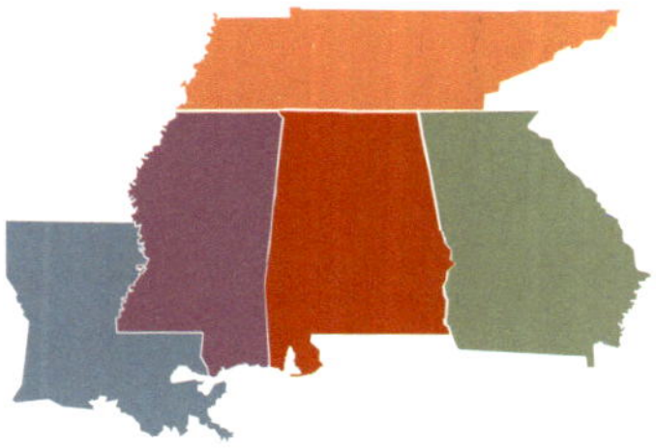

Introduction

Rug Hooking in THE DEEP SOUTH

Alabama, Louisiana, Mississippi, Tennessee, and Georgia; the five states of The Deep South. Grits, gumbo, and *Gone with the Wind*. Civil War and Civil Rights. Ancient oaks draped in Spanish moss. And high speed beltways. Riverboats lazily cruise that "Ol' Man River" against a backdrop of towering glass and steel. Chattanooga, Savannah, Atlanta, and Baton Rouge. Mobile, Montgomery, and Memphis; Jackson, Natchez and New Orleans. These cities of culture and hubs of industry offer the best of the both worlds. The old South and the new South…but always and forever…The Deep South. Living is easy and the weather is warm. No need to hand-hook rugs for cold and drafty floors.

And yet there is an ever increasing number of people in these warm Southern states who hook rugs. Hooking, a craft typically associated with colder climes, has struck a high note with many living in The Deep South – native born and newcomers alike. Drawn to this stress-reducing art form, often referred to as painting with wool, and the camaraderie of fellow enthusiasts, record numbers of hooked rugs are being made in Alabama, Louisiana, Mississippi, Tennessee, and Georgia. Such proficiency dispels the notion that hand-made rugs are only created by grandmothers living in New England and Canada. Take a look. The hooking artists of The Deep South, past and present, will impress and delight you… and do it ASAP…As Southern As Possible.

NOTE:
Hooked rug measurements have been rounded to the nearest half-inch. All rugs are hooked on burlap, rug hooking linen, monk's cloth, cotton warp, or other foundations using cut strips of woolen fabric unless noted. In some cases of special interest, the hooking materials have been listed. Using information supplied by rug owners as well as my own research, all efforts have been made to properly identify rug hookers, titles of their work, dates of completion, dimensions, and names of patterns and pattern makers. The author claims no responsibility for any misidentification. All hooked pieces adapted from the work of other artists were done so with permission. Permission was obtained by the hooking artist and not the author. The author accepts no responsibility for any copyright infringements.

THE QUEST FOR HOOKING SUPPLIES

Wool fabric is the preferred material for hooking. Typically one does not associate The Deep South with wool. Cotton... yes. Wool...no. So when it comes to finding their wools Southern rug hookers must be extra diligent. A determined Wilma Hill, who learned to hook while living in Chattanooga, Tennessee, expressed her feelings in "Wool Gathering." Moving to Baton Rouge, Louisiana, she opened a rug studio and taught hooking to hundreds of students over the next twenty plus years.

Wilma loves to hook and she knows how to find wool.

Wool Gathering

Wilma Hill

Please take time to read this - you must understand;
A new kind of "woolly worm" has invaded our land!
You're apt to encounter one any old place,
But never be fooled by the kind, friendly face.

For hidden within each mild beating heart
Is a burning desire to further their art.
The calm, outward appearance hides a tempest within;
They're certain the one with the most wool wins!

They begin to collect in the most innocent ways,
Taking only enough to last a few days.
But as they sit down with their work late one night,
They discover the colors they have aren't quite right.

They're missing a green or a blue – what a pain!
And they vow it will never happen again.
What began as a fun and leisure time pleasure
Turns into a quest for more woolen treasure.

At first it may be just a few extra strips,
Thinking to save some between lesson trips.
But take it from one, who happens to know,
The stash starts to grow, and to grow and to grow.

With olive and gray green no longer content,
They now must add teal, juniper, and mint.
And, oh yes, a plain color is no longer hip;
They've discovered the casserole, spot dye and dip!

They keep adding swatches and notches and more;
They carry big bags as they go out the door.
You'll find them at flea markets, Goodwill and such;
Their closets are full, there's simply too much.

And soon they can't live on just wool alone;
They must have the dyes to create their own.
So next comes the dye pots, jars and big pans,
And yardage in off-white, pastels and tans.

A bolt of old ivory, a plaid in light pink,
And stacks of those wonderful tweeds, so they think.
They have so much wool within their possession,
It's no longer a hobby – it's now an obsession!

Yet they crave more, considerably more;
Why, some even travel to buy it from Dorr!
The term wool gathering doesn't seem to begin
To cover the plight these junkies are in.

Is there not help for these poor souls, you say?
Would an army of great hungry moths save the day?
I wish I could offer a simple solution,
A way to reach some good resolution.

But I cannot, you see, for I'm off right away;
I hear there's a sale on wool fabric today!
I must get there first and pick out the best,
And then you are welcome to have all the rest!

Chapter 1

Sweet Home ALABAMA

Alabama is the deepest part of The Deep South, where the heart of Dixie beats strong and true and Jefferson Davis's birthday is a celebrated holiday. Hickory smoked barbecue, corn bread, and plenty of tea are on the menu. The living is easy in the state where cotton was king. Rich in history, Alabama is also home to NASA's Marshall Space Flight Center where the latest technology is developed to send men and women to the moon and beyond.

Many in the "Camellia State" have embraced the tradition of rug hooking. Among those most enthusiastic are members of The Heart of Dixie Rug Bees. Their work, and that of fellow Alabama rug hookers, is featured in this chapter.

Becki Cumbie

A hooking artist at work; Becki Cumbie hones her craft. Alabama. 2008. *Courtesy of Becki Cumbie*.

As a pottery collector, Becki Cumbie's attention was drawn to "Yellow Ware Crows," a hooked rug pattern she spotted while browsing a Nova Scotia web site. The Canadian design headed south, underwent a few minor changes and now adds a note of cheer to Becki's Alabama home. Wild Cranberry Hooked Rugs. Original pattern by Cynthia H. Black. Hooked by Becki Cumbie. Alabama. 2006. 18" x 26". *Courtesy of Becki Cumbie*

"I planned this rug when I learned that our son had gotten orders to serve in Iraq. I thought I could better deal with my worry while hooking so the idea of a 'family story' rug began to take shape. My husband and I built our log house 20 years ago. The yellow ribbon and the flag are to remember our son in the Middle East and the three gold stars represent our daughter, our other son, and daughter-in law." "Home." Designed by Becki Cumbie and her daughter, Haley. Hooked by Becki Cumbie. Alabama. 2008. 23" x 29". *Courtesy of Becki Cumbie.*

Inspired by an old oil painting, Beverly St. Clair hooked "Under the Stars." The captured moment of moon, stars and midnight gazers is a hauntingly serene scene. In addition to hooking with cut strips of woolen fabric, Beverly used metallic yarns to create sparkling stars and also added jewel-like snowflake adornments. Designed and hooked by Beverly St. Clair. Alabama. 2007. 16.5" x 14.5". *Courtesy of Beverly St. Clair*.

"My son lives in the Florida Panhandle where the water is a beautiful blue-green and the sand is very white. 'Kaleidoscope' was a birthday gift for him because the colors reminded me of that area." Designed by Jane Olson. Hooked by Beverly St. Clair. Alabama. 2007. 42" x 30". *Courtesy of Beverly St. Clair.*

"Yard of Gardens," complete with raised and sculptured hooked flowers and shrubs, is every botanist's dream cottage. Pattern maker unknown. Hooked by Beverly St. Clair. Alabama. 1995. 10" x 35.5". *Courtesy of Beverly St. Clair.*

A whipped stitch edging complements six ornate "Medallion" squares. Designed by Jane McGown Flynn. House of Price / Charco pattern. Hooked by Beverly St. Clair. Alabama. 2005. 26" x 38.5". *Courtesy of Beverly St. Clair.*

"Tapestry Bunnies" play among the flowers growing on a crazed field. True to their heritage, the hooked hares are ornately contained, tasseled and ready to hang on your castle wall. "'Tapestry Bunnies' was started at Castle in the Clouds Rug School. Jessie Turbayne was there that year and saw the bunnies and mentioned the names Edgar and Wilbur. I put their names next to them on this wall hanging as a remembrance of her checking out my rabbits." (Author's note: Spending many happy times at Castle in the Clouds Rug Hooking School, I have fond memories of the students, teachers, and the school's late founder and director, Chattanooga's own Ramona Maddox. I am delighted to see Beverly's finished work, complete with the names I jokingly bestowed on the hare pair.) Designed by Victoria Hart Ingalls. Hooked by Beverly St. Clair. Alabama. 1998. 25.5" x 33.5". *Courtesy of Beverly St. Clair.*

Utilizing Jeanne Benjamin's popular "Crow Feathers" dyed wool, Beverly St. Clair fashioned "Bird Vest." "I have been questioned about what the birds are and I know that, somewhere in the world, there is a bird that looks like one on my vest!" In addition to hooking with strips of woolen fabric, metallic yarns were used for accents. Designed and hooked by Beverly St. Clair. Alabama. 2002. *Courtesy of Beverly St. Clair.*

Hooking lends its self to many things other than rugs and wall hangings. Come Christmas, this trio of three-dimensional Santas is put on display for all to enjoy. Designed and hooked by Beverly St. Clair. Alabama. 2003. The three large Santas are 11" tall. The small Santa is 7" tall. *Courtesy of Beverly St. Clair*

An ornate wrought iron entryway inspired "Eden's Gate." Eighteen "critters" dwell within a mystical hooked world. Designed and hooked by Beverly St. Clair. Alabama. 2000. 45" x 34". *Courtesy of Beverly St. Clair.*

Using left over scraps, Beverly St. Clair hooked "Mille Fleur," a rug that "looks great anywhere." Designed by Jane McGown Flynn. House of Price / Charco pattern. Hooked by Beverly St. Clair. Alabama. 2007. 27" x 45". *Courtesy of Beverly St. Clair.*

Butterflies and blue bird are attracted to a vibrant overflowing basket of summer's bounty. The picket fence-like border, with lamb's tongue detail, frames three quarters of "A Tapestry of Memories." This popular design was also available as a jig saw puzzle. "The hooking was easier and much more fun than the puzzle." Designed by Gary Head. Hooked by Beverly St. Clair. 2002. Alabama. 20.5" x 27.5". *Courtesy of Beverly St. Clair.*

"Chinese Roundel" graces the ceiling of Beverly St. Clair's home. This eye-catching kaleidoscope medallion, hooked in jewel-like tones, is the focal point of her living room. Designed by Jane McGown Flynn. House of Price / Charco pattern. Hooked by Beverly St. Clair. Alabama. 1995. Diameter 36". *Courtesy of Beverly St. Clair.*

"This book bag was made for my daughter who is a teacher. She teaches a Shakespeare class for high school seniors. *Little Women* and *To Kill a Mockingbird* are two of her favorite books." Designed and hooked by Beverly St. Clair. Alabama. 1995. 18" x 17". *Courtesy of Beverly St. Clair.*

Dean Black

"Basket Weave Hit and Miss" composed of bulging striped bands of color, reminds one of overstuffed upholstery webbing. "This rug was supposed to be squares. I don't know why it came out with the curves but I like it." "Packing" too many hooked loops into the outlines of the squares created curves. The curves create a pleasing optical illusion of depth. Designed and hooked by Dean Black. Alabama. 2005. 39" x 44". *Courtesy of Dean Black.*

Perched on their red bench and immortalized in this primitive-style hooked rug are brother and sister felines, Pepper and Tiny. Living in a log home and possessing a love for things from the past, Dean Black became interested in hooked rugs while working in an antique shop. "Black Cats" designed by Pat Hornafius. Hooked by Dean Black. Alabama. 2005. 24" x 36". *Courtesy of Dean Black.*

Three vibrant "Stars" dance upon a mottled field of deep crimson. Concentric rectangles frame the lively trio. Designed and hooked by Dean Black. Alabama. 2004. 23" x 36". *Courtesy of Dean Black.*

Typically crafted from appliquéd pieces of fabric, this "Penny Runner" was hooked and made to grace a special table. An antique black background makes the colors of the circles, flowers and fan details "pop." Designed by Sally Van Nuys. Hooked by Dean Black. Alabama. 2007. 13.5" x 41". *Courtesy of Dean Black.*

A footstool purchased in a Georgia antique shop was the perfect fit for "Bluebirds and Berries." Adapted from the pattern "Quilted Cats" by Pat Cross. Hooked by Dean Black. Alabama. 2008. 7" x 12". *Courtesy of Dean Black.*

"'Fantasy Garden Tote' was a pleasure to hook and is a pleasure to use." Primitive vines and flowers surround a foraging feathered friend. Designed by Susan Quicksall. Hooked by Dean Black. Alabama. 2007. 9" x 13.5". *Courtesy of Dean Black.*

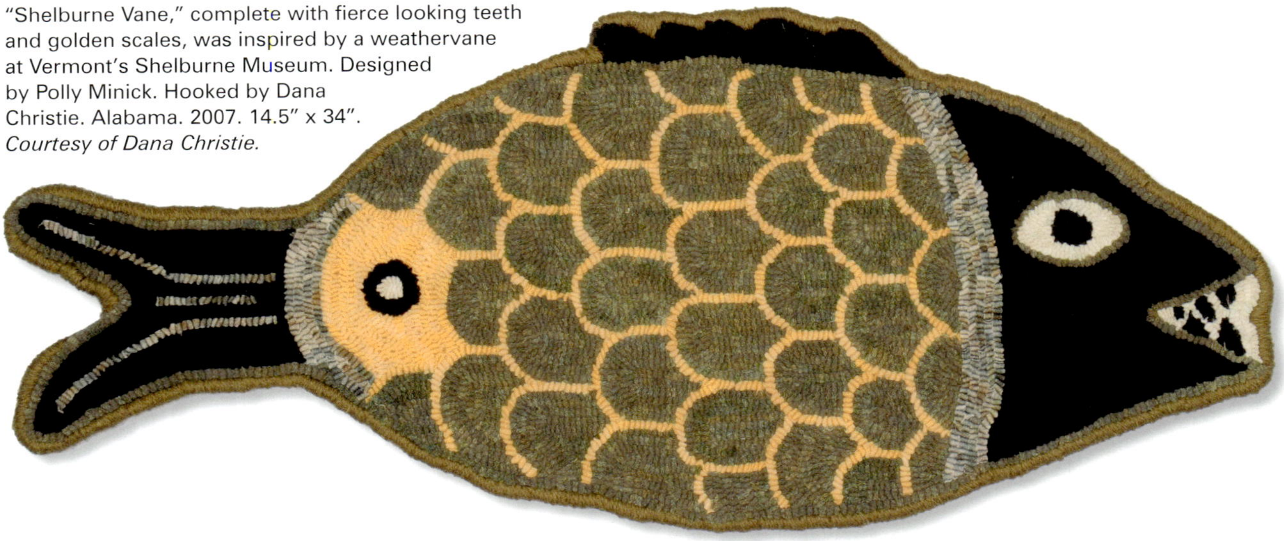

"Shelburne Vane," complete with fierce looking teeth and golden scales, was inspired by a weathervane at Vermont's Shelburne Museum. Designed by Polly Minick. Hooked by Dana Christie. Alabama. 2007. 14.5" x 34". *Courtesy of Dana Christie.*

Pleasant Dreams. "This 'Bed Bug Rug' was made for my husband and lies by the side of his bed. And each night before going to sleep he is reminded, 'Don't let the bed bugs bite.'" Designed and hooked by Dana Christie. Alabama. 2004. 26" x 26". *Courtesy of Dana Christie.*

Hooked for a best friend's 50th birthday and named for the trees that surround the property, "White Oak" welcomes all to a beloved home. Designed and hooked by Dana Christie. Alabama. 2008. 19" x 24". *Courtesy of Dana Christie.*

A 50th birthday gift for Dana Christie's brother, "Queen of the Sea" glides through the water, starfish in hand. Cactus Needle pattern. Hooked by Dana Christie. Alabama. 2006. 14" x 30". *Courtesy of Dana Christie*.

Big, bold, and brilliant blossoms spring forth from an "Old Pot," folk art with a modern twist. M. Hoops / Fleecewood pattern. Hooked by Dana Christie. Alabama. 2005. 27" x 37". *Courtesy of Dana Christie.*

"Primitive is my style. I was just practicing to keep a straight line. It is a year later and my lines still are not straight and never will be but that's OK with me. What fun!" "3 Square Pillow" in a rectangular shape. Designed and hooked by Diana McMichen. Alabama. 2007. 10" x 21". *Courtesy of Diana McMichen*.

"Sampler Purse" was a practice piece for a new hooker. Hit or miss stripes, circles, and a star come together and form a delightful tote. Designed and hooked by Diana McMichen. Alabama. 2007. 12" x 12". *Courtesy of Diana McMichen.*

A hooked flower adds a pop of color to "My Hooking Bag." A real attention getter. "When I am waiting in line at stores my purse always gets noticed." Designed and hooked by Diana McMichen. Alabama. 2007. 16.5" x 16". *Courtesy of Diana McMichen.*

The backside of the aforementioned "My Hooking Bag" complete with old buttons and a handy pocket. Designed and hooked by Diana McMichen. Alabama. 2007. 16.5" x 16". *Courtesy of Diana McMichen.*

"This rug was to be a hit or miss pattern. Bored after four squares I decided to put an 'artsy' touch to my primitive design and add the saying 'Give Thanks.' I could not get the 'S' to fit into the square, so I used the whole empty square next to it!" Designed and hooked by Diana McMichen. Alabama. 2008. 19" x 52". *Courtesy of Diana McMichen.*

A blue suited Santa, complete with decorated Christmas tree, is surrounded by circles of concentric design. Konfetti's K102 Santa pattern. Hooked by Gloria Davis. Alabama. 2008. 13" x 12.5". *Courtesy of Gloria J. Davis.*

Hooked as master bedroom décor, "Long Stem Rose" rests on a vertically hooked green field. Adapted from an image found in a book. Designed and hooked by Gloria Davis. Alabama. 2006. 32" x 15.5". *Courtesy of Gloria J. Davis.*

Wanting to make brightly colored chair covers for her new dining room set, Gloria Davis hooked this floral design with strips of woolen fabric. She then used yarn to hook the background. Pearl McGown pattern. Hooked by Gloria Davis. Alabama. 2008. 16.5" x 14". *Courtesy of Gloria J. Davis.*

A treasured heirloom, colorful abstract flowers surround a central motif of hands, hearts, and intertwining ribbon. "I have three grandchildren that the 'Hands' represent. The fourth hand is for the fourth child should we be so blessed." Adapted from a pattern found in *Rug Hooking* magazine. Hooked by Gloria Davis. Alabama. 2007. 30.5" x 27.5". *Courtesy of Gloria J. Davis.*

Hestel Broome

A mother, grandmother, and great grandmother, Hestel Broome paints on canvas and china, and, once a week, hooks with friends. When it comes to rug hooking she has mastered the art of fine shading. To achieve such realistic detail rug hookers use finely woven woolen fabric cut into strips 3/32" and 4/32" wide. Pictured is "Fruit Chair Seat," one in a series. Pearl McGown pattern. Hooked by Hestel Broome. Alabama. 1986. Diameter 14". *Courtesy of Hestel Broome.*

Painting with wool. Another in the "Fruit Chair Seat" series. Pearl McGown pattern. Hooked by Hestel Broome. Alabama. 1986. Diameter 14". *Courtesy of Hestel Broome.*

Hestel Broome's china painting abilities are reflected in her hooked art. "Iris and Pussy Willow" is a delicate hooked floral still life, reminiscent of images found on Auntie's favorite bone china teacups. Jacqueline Hansen Designs. Hooked by Hestel Broome. Alabama. 1987. Diameter 14". *Courtesy of Hestel Broome*

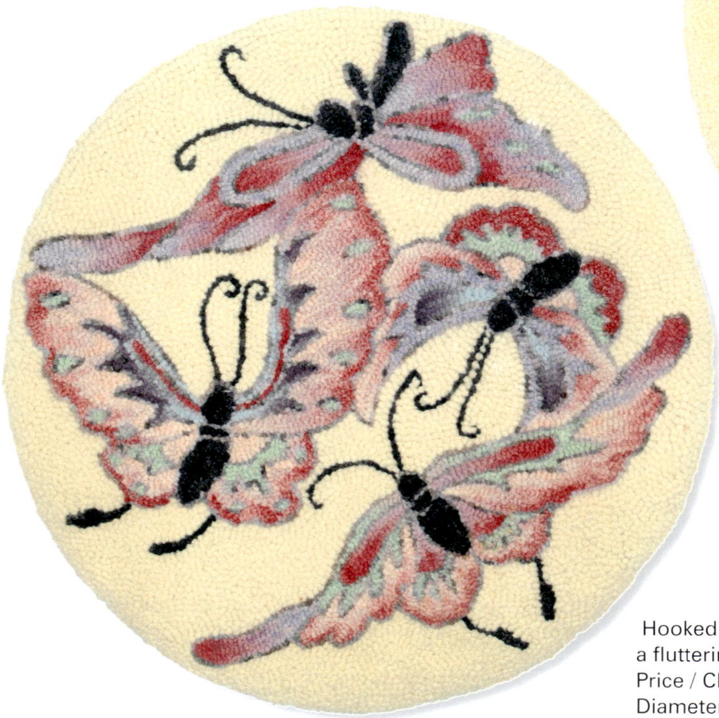

Hooked in a pleasing pastel palette, "Oriental Butterfly" captures a fluttering foursome. Designed by Jane McGown Flynn. House of Price / Charco pattern. Hooked by Hestel Broome. Alabama. 1995. Diameter 15". *Courtesy of Hestel Broome.*

What a delight to rest your feet on a hooked bouquet of tulips, iris, morning glory, dogwood, and forget-me-nots. "Floral Footstool." Designed and hooked by Hestel Broome. Alabama. 2001. 9.5" x 15". *Courtesy of Hestel Broome.*

"Rosmaling," a Scandinavian style of painting found on walls, furniture, and wooden dinnerware, inspires both rug hookers and patterns makers. "Rosmaling Footstool." Jacqueline Hansen Design. Hooked by Hestel Broome. Alabama. 1996. 13.5" x 16.5". *Courtesy of Hestel Broome.*

"I had never painted a portrait, but thought perhaps I could hook one. The hair was easy. The eyes were a challenge." "Gibson Girl." Adapted from a picture in *Antiques* magazine. Hooked by Hestel Broome. Alabama. 1999. 19" x 13". *Courtesy of Hestel Broome*.

An ornate frame complements a skillfully crafted "English Cottage." Hestel Broome's horizontally hooked grass mimics the flat plane of the lawn and accentuates curves of the walkway, mounds of flowers, and background trees. A mottled, pearl-like sky highlights this quaint thatched home. Adapted from "Yard of Gardens." Prairie Craft House pattern. Hooked by Hestel Broome. Alabama. 2002. 13" x 16". *Courtesy of Hestel Broome.*

"Feathered Friends," in the cat o' nine tails, are posed against a painted sky. Jacqueline Hansen Designs. Hooked by Hestel Broome. Alabama. 2005. 14.5" x 12". *Courtesy of Hestel Broome.*

Tiny hooked loops form a tiny feline face. "Kitten with Violets." Victoria Hart Ingalls pattern. Hooked by Hestel Broome. Alabama. 1997. Diameter 9.5". *Courtesy of Hestel Broome.*

"Alexandra;" a detailed and dainty floral bouquet is hooked, framed and ready to hang. Rittermere pattern. Hooked by Hestel Broome. Alabama. 1985. 19" x 15". *Courtesy of Hestel Broome.*

"Patience" is what it took to hook this finely shaded study of rose, daisy, and morning glory. The finished piece was fashioned into a decorative accent pillow. Designed by Jane McGown Flynn. House of Price / Charco pattern. Hooked by Hestel Broome. Alabama. 1989. Diameter 12". *Courtesy of Hestel Broome.*

Imogene Hand

Flowing lines, floral motifs, and angular accents, hooked in vibrant color make for a delightful Persian-style rug. New Earth Designs pattern. Hooked by Imogene Hand. Alabama. 2001. 24" x 38". *Courtesy of Imogene Hand.*

Jacque Juvenal

A fine-feathered fowl, "Just Sitting" but decked out in jewels and ready to party. "My whimsy working overtime. She's a hit around here at Mardi Gras!" Jane McGown Flynn pattern. House of Price / Charco pattern. Hooked by Jacque Juvenal. Alabama. 2002. 16.5 x 15". *Courtesy of Jacque Juvenal.*

"Happy Everything" celebrates it all! Halloween, Santa, birthday cupcakes, a four- leaf clover personalized for a special granddaughter and more. If it's a special event Jacque Juvenal has it covered. Her holiday free-for-all is embellished with wool roving, feathers, and metallic threads. Designed by Betty Lew. Hooked by Jacque Juvenal. Alabama. 2006. 66" x 21". *Courtesy of Jacque Juvenal.*

Far left:
Embroidered chair seat designs inspired "Jacque's Crewel." The carved wooden hanger, originally from a convent in Missouri, adds a functioning and finishing touch to this hooked Jacobean-style banner. Designed by Jane McGown Flynn. House of Price / Charco pattern. Hooked by Jacque Juvenal. Alabama. 1985. 36" x 13". *Courtesy of Jacque Juvenal.*

Left:
Tribute is paid to the raised and sculptured hooked rugs of Waldoboro, Maine, and Waldoboro hooking master Jacqueline Hansen. Jackie Juvenal's raised hooking enhanced the cleavage of "Mermaid" to the point that comment was made that her rug needed a bra. This devilish dame of the deep, complete with a be-jeweled navel, now hangs in Jacque's husband's bathroom where she is viewed and enjoyed on a regular basis. Designed by Kris Miller / Spruce Ridge Studios. Hooked by Jacque Juvenal. Alabama. 2005. 55" x 22". *Courtesy of Jacque Juvenal.*

"Delicious Dozen" makes for a charming table-top runner. Note the fine shading in both the fruit and foliage. Designed by Jane McGown Flynn. House of Price / Charco pattern. Hooked by Jacque Juvenal. Alabama. 1998. 11.5" x 42". *Courtesy of Jacque Juvenal.*

"Peruvian Images" was an enjoyable class project partly because of the research. "This rug made me wish I was in Lima, the City of Kings." Geometric elements combine with mythical-like fish, two-headed serpents, and coupled birds. Designed by Jane McGown Flynn. House of Price / Charco pattern. Hooked by Jacque Juvenal. Alabama. 1994. 52" x 32". *Courtesy of Jacque Juvenal.*

"People ask how long it took me to finish 'The Carolers' – I always say ten years because I was only working two or three weeks per year." A true holiday project. Margaret Hunt Masters pattern. Hooked by Jacque Juvenal. Alabama. 1992. 42" x 66". *Courtesy of Jacque Juvenal.*

A bare footed "Little Bo Peep" merrily leads her sheep away from towering stalks of abstract flowers. The curly coats of the foursome were hooked with gray, natural, and black wool roving. Quail Hill Designs. Hooked by Jacque Juvenal. Alabama. 2003. 27" x 39". *Courtesy of Jacque Juvenal.*

With a wardrobe hooked from a variety of plaids, "'The Ring' honors my five friends. Since finishing this project two of my very close friends have left for the golden hook in the sky." Pris Buttler Rug Designs. Hooked by Jacque Juvenal. Alabama. 2005. Diameter 32". *Courtesy of Jacque Juvenal.*

"This rug, a labor of love, was made to commemorate my husband Mike's 50th reunion at West Point. The center motif is the academy's emblem flanked by crests of the class of 1952, one bearing Mike's initials. A chain, once stretched across the Hudson River to keep the Brits out, forms the rug's outer border. The somber background shade of gray was chosen to represent the harshness of winter. Admired by many, this special rug made the trip to the reunion and someday, honoring Mike's wish, will grace the West Point Museum." Designed and hooked by Jacque Juvenal. Alabama. 2001. 61" x 34". *Courtesy of Jacque Juvenal.*

"'Where's Harriet' was a fun rug to do. I really didn't want to finish it as I had so much fun doing the little people." Included in the joyful crowd are vintage Hollywood actress Jane Withers on roller skates, Harry Potter, Pippi Long Stockings, a Red Sox fan, and assorted family members. Someone must be named Harriet! Patsy Becker pattern. Hooked by Jacque Juvenal. Alabama. 2009. 40" x 29". *Courtesy of Jacque Juvenal.*

Liz Philbrick

"Antique Pineapple" is a popular pattern that combines twin symbols of welcome with primitive flowers and vines. Hooking artist Liz Philbrick used wool skirts and shirts over-dyed with complementary colors, giving her rug a vintage look. Quail Hill Designs. Hooked by Liz Philbrick. Alabama. 2005. 36" x 70". *Courtesy of Liz Philbrick.*

When the temperatures soar, this southern rug hooker heads north to Lake Champlain. "'Summers in Vermont' shows the beautifully, incredibly starry skies and the homes of the two Rose families from whom we rent a cottage. Ours is the one on the left. I hoped to capture the memories of those evenings in this rug, and I think I have. Also it is here that I started hooking after seeing some beautiful Vermont rugs at a fair." A brilliant full moon illuminates the charming scene. Note Liz Philbrick's initials and date hooked into the night sky. Designed and hooked by Liz Philbrick. Alabama. 2003. 33" x 35". *Courtesy of Liz Philbrick.*

This rug started out as a pattern with pine trees. Hooking pinecones proved to be a tad bit difficult so Liz Philbrick went floral and things ended up smelling like roses..." Eight Roses." Adapted from "Bigelow Pine." Harry M. Fraser Co. pattern. Hooked by Liz Philbrick. Alabama. 2008. 32" x 58". *Courtesy of Liz Philbrick.*

"My granddaughter Claudia always loved the song 'Twinkle, Twinkle Little Star.' Her mother sang it to her at night and other times to calm her down. Her last name being Sparks I changed the words of the song to make it hers, and to endow a little wisdom." Knowing of Claudia's love of the constellations, Grandmother Liz hooked in a night sky. "The Ring." Pris Buttler Rug Designs. Hooked by Liz Philbrick. Alabama. 2004. Diameter 34". *Courtesy of Liz Philbrick.*

Honoring a new son-in-law's Scottish and Irish heritage, Liz Philbrick hooked a "Wedding Rug for Clay and Melissa." The happy couple exchanged vows and Claddagh rings while standing on this special gift. Designed and hooked by Liz Philbrick. Alabama. 2004. 32" x 46". *Courtesy of Liz Philbrick.*

Even distribution of color makes for an aesthetically pleasing rug. The vibrant hand-dyed wools that were used to hook "Primitive Fruit" also appear in the outer hit or miss striped border. House of Price / Charco pattern. Hooked by Liz Philbrick. Alabama. 2003. 25" x 44". *Courtesy of Liz Philbrick.*

Reaching for the sun, over-sized blooms and blossoms protect a little red house where, as indicated by the heart carved into the garden gate, love abounds. "A Towne Garden." Karen Kahle / Primitive Spirit pattern. Hooked by Liz Philbrick. Alabama. 2002. 32" x 30". *Courtesy of Liz Philbrick.*

Louise Wilson

Finely shaded "Old Rose," is a hooked study of the beloved symbol of love and romance. Victoria Hart Ingalls pattern. Hooked by Louise Wilson. Alabama. 2007. 17" x 17". *Courtesy of Louise Wilson.*

Linda Zannetti

"Gabby 'adopted' us in September of 1996. Although he grew to 24" long (excluding his tail) and weighed over 20 lbs, he was the most gentle 'giant' and our baby. We lost him in October of 2000 but he still remains in our minds and in our hearts." The pattern for "Gabby" was made by transferring a photo image onto rug warp. Hooked by Linda Zannetti. Alabama. 2003. 18" x 14.5". *Courtesy of Linda Zannetti.*

Granddaughter Crystal collects anything "zebra"... so, of course, Linda Zannetti hooked her a striped friend using shades of brown, six shades of white, and six shades of black. Designed by Sibyl Osicka. Hooked by Linda Zannetti. Alabama. 2005. 24" x 20". *Courtesy of Linda Zannetti.*

Mary Jo Dorning

A love for "Americana" inspired Mary Jo Dorning to hook "The Little Patriot." Starting in 1974 when a friend invited her to a hooking class, she has been hooking ever since. Victoria Hart Ingalls pattern. Hooked by Mary Jo Dorning. Alabama. 2000. 20" x 24". *Courtesy of Mary Jo Dorning.*

"I saw 'Two Roosters' in *Early American Life* and fell in love with it." The accompanying article discussed natural dyeing so Mary Jo Dorning put her pots on the stove and dyed woolen fabric with mimosa leaves, walnuts, and golden rod. The pleasing results complement a proud barnyard pair. Designed by Pat Hornafius. Hooked by Mary Jo Dorning. Alabama. 2004. 24" x 34". *Courtesy of Mary Jo Dorning.*

A white Christmas in The Deep South. "I had to hook 'Mammy's House' because it depicts my family home where so many fond memories were had, especially at holiday times. My mom and dad (Mammy and Pappy) are gone now and others live in the house, yet my heartfelt memories are as vivid as ever in this piece." Although a rare occurrence, Mary Jo Dorning recalls a blizzard that dumped 18" of snow on her Birmingham, Alabama, childhood home. Designed and hooked by Mary Jo Dorning. Alabama. 2000. 29" x 35". *Courtesy of Mary Jo Dorning.*

Craving snow and ice, Deep South hooking artist Mary Jo Dorning crafted "Neighborhood Skaters." "I thought it was about the prettiest thing I had ever seen." Designed by Margaret Hunt Masters. Hooked by Mary Jo Dorning. Alabama. 1999. 31" x 46". *Courtesy of Mary Jo Dorning.*

The "Lion and Lamb" reminds us of the Biblical story that teaches love and compassion. A scalloped border frames the tranquil duo. Designed by Jane McGown Flynn. House of Price / Charco pattern. Hooked by Mary Jo Dorning. Alabama. 1995. 26" x 42". *Courtesy of Mary Jo Dorning*

"I grew up with chickens and loved going in my grandmother's hen house. This little rug appealed to me and brought back memories of her." "Hen." Lib Callaway patterns. Hooked by Mary Jo Dorning. Alabama. 1999. 30" x 40". *Courtesy of Mary Jo Dorning.*

Adapted from an antique quilt, Mary Jo Dorning hooked a folk art "Bicentennial America," rug complete with pineapples, houses, berries, floral motifs, and figures of George and Martha Washington. The First Couple are represented in the form of "Swedish silhouettes." Designed and hooked by Mary Jo Dorning. Alabama. 1992. 42" x 54". *Courtesy of Mary Jo Dorning.*

A work in progress, depicting an "East Machias," Maine village scene, finds its way to an Alabama rug hooking class. This unfinished hooked rug was purchased at a 2005 Alabama auction for $26. The winning bidder, Sheryl Bagley consulted a friend within her Needlepoint Guild and the project was turned over to Mary Jo Dorning to finish. Designed by Edith Dana. Started by an unknown rug hooker and completed by Mary Jo Dorning. Alabama. 2008. 38" x 72". *Courtesy of Mary Jo Dorning and Sheryl S. Bagley.*

Mary Jo Dorning at work. Alabama. 2008. *Courtesy of Mary Jo Dorning*.

The hooked "East Michias" Maine village scene is completed and ready for hanging in an Alabama home. Hooked by Mary Jo Dorning. Alabama. 2008. 38" x 72". *Courtesy of Mary Jo Dorning and Sheryl S. Bagley.*

Melinda Dorning

While living in Alabama, Melinda was introduced to rug hooking by her mother-in-law Mary Jo Dorning. A trip to New York City with her husband Matt and a visit to an exhibit of vintage valentines at the Museum of American Folk Art inspired Melinda to hook "My Heart Is In Your Hand." Since relocating to Missouri this rug hooker has continued the family hooking tradition. Designed by Melinda and Matt Dorning. Hooked by Melinda Dorning. Missouri. 1992. 30" x 31". *Courtesy of Melinda Dorning*.

Miriam Rogers Fowler

Some projects just take a little longer than others. Started over 40 years ago, "Violets" was relegated to the back of a closet while life went on; children, back to work, back to college, two degrees, grandchildren, and two bouts of cancer. Now that Miriam is retired she hopes to finish her hooked floral fantasy in spite of having to reinforce the rug's aged burlap backing. "My next rug will be a Christmas rug, and, 'Lord willing,' it will not take 40 years." Designed by Rebecca Rugs. Hooked by Miriam Rogers Fowler. Alabama. 2008. A work in progress. 38" x 64". *Courtesy of Miriam Rogers Fowler.*

Marie Jeff

Motivated by Bible stories, folk and fairy tales, hooking artist Marie Jeff designs all her rugs from her own original drawings. She utilizes old woolen clothing cut by hand into hook-able strips; some dyed with natural materials. Here displayed before being "baked in a pie" are "Four and Twenty Black Birds" complemented with corner notes of their royal song. Designed and hooked by Marie Jeff. Alabama. 1993. 33.5" x 46". *Courtesy of Marie Jeff.*

A leering snake, hooked from metallic braid, threatens "Adam and Eve" as they seek cover behind a tree laden with ripe apples. Designed and hooked by Marie Jeff. Alabama. 1994. 38.5" x 44". *Courtesy of Marie Jeff*

Noah, dressed in yellow rain gear, welcomes silhouetted pairs of animals onto his ark as doves secure a storm warning flag above. Open umbrellas decorate the corners and re-enforce the prediction of foul weather ahead. "Noah and the Ark." Designed and hooked by Marie Jeff. Alabama. 1996. 39" x 56". *Courtesy of Marie Jeff.*

Marie Jeff created "The Lion and the Lamb" as a tribute to a favorite Bible story. Her king of beast, bold in color and design, shares the scene with a petite lamb and golden bird. An equally bold geometric border complements the scene. Designed and hooked by Marie Jeff. Alabama. 1987. 35" x 47". *Courtesy of Marie Jeff.*

Jonah learns a hard lesson on rough seas. "Jonah and the Whale." Designed and hooked by Marie Jeff. Alabama. 1988. 36" x 54.5". *Courtesy of Marie Jeff.*

Marie Jeff hooked a portrait of "Br'er Rabbit," the beloved trickster from the Uncle Remus stories first published in the South in 1881. Succeeding through his wits, this bunny poses behind twisting and turning briars. Designed and hooked by Marie Jeffs. Alabama. 1991.37.5" x 50". *Courtesy of Marie Jeff.*

A sound piece of advice to all from a trio of impish monkeys. Often attributed to an ancient Japanese proverb, Marie Jeff hooked "See No Evil, Hear No Evil, Speak No Evil." Designed and hooked by Marie Jeff. Alabama. 1989. 37" x 54". *Courtesy of Marie Jeff.*

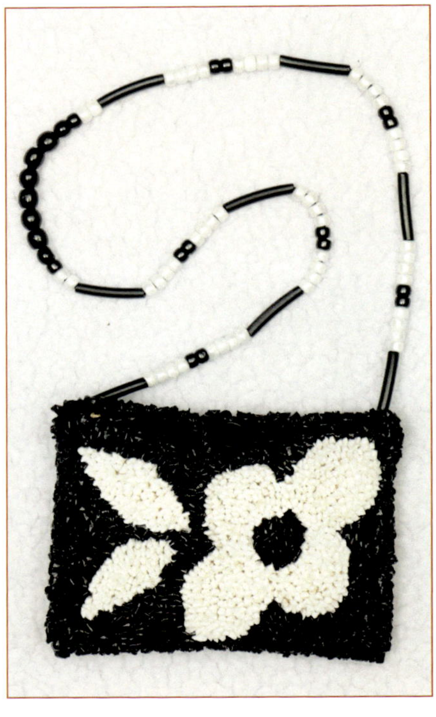

Exploring a different avenue of hooking Marie Jeff created an original "Black and White Purse" using cut up strips of plastic bags. A strap of beads completes the fashion statement. Designed and hooked by Marie Jeff. Alabama. 2007. 5.5" x 7.5". *Courtesy of Marie Jeff.*

Nell Staab

Right:
Years back Nell Staab started hooking with a friend whose son was stationed in Viet Nam. She lost interest and her "Strawberry" rug was put aside for 30 years. Time passed until, "I found a group of hookers and finished it in 2000!" Six vine formed blocks hold two ripe strawberries and a trio of white flowers that sparkle like jewels against a dark background. Pattern maker unknown. Hooked by Nell Staab. Alabama. 2000. 45" x 31". *Courtesy of Nell Staab.*

Functional and fashionable; "Clam Shell Tote." This class project serves two purposes. Designed by Jacque Juvenal and Anne Mather. Hooked by Nell Staab. Alabama. 2005. 15.5" x 13". *Courtesy of Nell Staab.*

Pat Martin

After seeing a young woman carrying a purse adapted from an American flag, Pat Martin picked up her hook, selected patriotic, re-cycled wool fabric and went to work hooking her own "Flag Purse." Designed and hooked by Pat Martin. Alabama. 2001. 9.5" x 11". *Courtesy of Pat Martin.*

The always popular "Vermont Shell" pattern is right at home in Alabama. Pearl McGown pattern. Hooked by Pat Martin. Alabama. 1996. 28" x 41". *Courtesy of Pat Martin.*

Pat Martin's very first hooking project, "Porcelain Cat" recalls prized collectible figurines. Designed by Jane McGown Flynn. House of Price / Charco pattern. Hooked by Pat Martin. Alabama. 1995. 18" x 30". *Courtesy of Pat Martin.*

A festive hooked stocking with three-dimensional poinsettias awaits the arrival of Santa on Christmas Eve. Designed by Gene Shepherd. Hooked by Ginger Thomas. Alabama. 2008. 21" tall. *Courtesy of Ginger Thomas*.

Every rug hooker's best friend, "McDuff." His curly coat was achieved by hooking with a variety of yarns. Designed by Jane McGown Flynn. House of Price / Charco pattern. Hooked by Ginger Thomas. Alabama. 2007. 15" x 16". *Courtesy of Ginger Thomas.*

Some rug hookers find both spiritual and physical comfort in the work they do. "Cabin Repeat Pillow," a favorite quilt pattern, is enriched by touches of golden yellow. Designed by Jane McGown Flynn. House of Price / Charco pattern. Hooked by Ginger Thomas. Alabama. 2008. 12" x 12". *Courtesy of Ginger Thomas*.

"Stained Glass Santa" took several years to complete but the finished product was well worth the wait. Ginger Thomas embellished this jolly old fellow with wool roving, decorative threads, assorted Christmas themed buttons, and braided yarn trim. Designed by Carol Kassera. Hooked by Ginger Thomas. Alabama. 2008. 20" x 13". *Courtesy of Ginger Thomas*.

"Ramona's Garden," completed with raised and sculptured hooked flowers, was fashioned in memory of the late Ramona Maddox, a rug hooking artist, teacher, and dear friend to many, including Ginger Thomas and this author. In addition to her rug making talents Ramona took great pride in the special garden she planted and tended at her Chattanooga home. Designed by Carol Kassera. Hooked by Ginger Thomas. Alabama. 2008. 11" x 12.5". *Courtesy of Ginger Thomas.*

Shelby Thomas

Hurricane Katrina may have displaced graduate student Shelby Thomas, but it led her to rug hooking. After moving back home to Alabama from New Orleans, Shelby accompanied her mother to hooking class and she, like her mother and aunt, became hooked. Pictured is an example of her creativity. An abstract, curlicue "S" design covers her hooked and monogrammed purse. Pattern by Faith Williston. Hooked by Shelby Thomas. Alabama. 2005. 12" x 18". *Courtesy of Shelby W. Thomas.*

Robin Duke

"The 'Twinkle Stars' pattern was my first rug. Of all the fiber arts, rug hooking is my favorite." Morton House Primitive pattern. Hooked by Robin Duke. Alabama. 1994. 19" x 25". *Courtesy of Robin Duke.*

A LOOK BACK:

The United States Home Extension Services, Rug Hooking, and Alabama

Anyone living in Alabama between the two World Wars was most likely familiar with the Home Demonstration Clubs. Sponsored by the United States Home Extension Services, female Home Demonstration agents reached out to women living in rural areas and offered them instruction in nutrition, hygiene, home making, child rearing, and cottage industry crafts. The destructive boll weevil and generation after generation of planting had left much of the Southern farmland depleted and useless. The Extension Services were a means of improving the lives of rural Southerners, including some who were without electrical service, telephones, and mail delivery.

Scattered throughout Alabama, Home Demonstration Clubs offered the buying public a variety of home-produced crafts, including pine straw baskets, tufted bed spreads, bath mats, kimonos, and rag rugs. Records from the 1920s, gathered by the Alabama Center for Traditional Culture, show women from several counties, including Barbour, Clay, Cullman, Escambia, Mobile, and Perry, were earning "significant amounts of money." Notation was also made of a woman from Cullman County who sold her hooked rugs for five dollars apiece and was helping the agent teach other women how to hook.

Thelma Bean

"Thelma Bean was a very talented and artistic person who loved doll making and rug hooking. She started rug hooking in the late 1940s or early 1950s with a Home Demonstration Club in Greenwood, Alabama and later on Cotton Avenue in Birmingham," recalls her daughter Linda Blass. Anyone living in Alabama between the two World Wars was familiar with Home Demonstration Clubs. Developed out of the United States Home Extension Services Female Home Demonstration agents reached out to women in the rural South trying to improve their lives by offering instruction in nutrition, hygiene, child-rearing, home-making and home produced crafts. An accomplished rug hooker, Thelma mastered fine tapestry-like shading using strips of wool fabric cut 4/32" wide. She passed away in June 2005 at the age of 91. Her daughter is the proud owner of this exquisite floral beauty. Pattern maker unknown. Hooked by Thelma Bean. Alabama. 1950s. Diameter 36". *Courtesy of Thelma Bean and Linda B. Blass.*

Chapter 2

LOUISIANA: The Melding of Cultures

Louisiana has a colorful history and a rich diversity of peoples. Being settled by the French, Spanish, West Indian, African, Irish, and Italian, Louisiana is now home to almost every nationality on earth. This blending of cultures creates an atmosphere for good times and good food. Bring on the gumbo, jambalaya, and étouffee. Faced with both natural and man-made disasters, such as Hurricane Katrina and the BP Gulf oil spill, Louisianans are an optimistic and resilient lot. Enjoy the Mardi Gras, jazz, and Cajun cuisine. The party never ends... when the Saints go marching in.

OLD SOUTH HOOKED RUG PATTERNS

Many rugs hooked in the 1940s were not merely floor coverings, but painstakingly planned and crafted still lifes in wool.

"Desire," designed and hooked by Marilyn Connor. *See page 54.*

Pictured on the cover of the 1948 copyrighted *Old South Hooked Rug Patterns,* and placed in front of a plantation rendering is "My Louisiana." Rug designer Francis C. Holden describes the popular pattern as "depicting native flowers and fruit of Louisiana with state flower, magnolias, predominating. Cotton bolls in corner."

Mrs. Francis C. Holden was a designer at the "Colonial Rug Shoppe" then located at 810 North Third Street in Monroe, Louisiana. Her *Old South Hooked Rug Patterns*, copyright 1948, was a popular source of inspiration for rug hookers living in the South and beyond. Included in her catalog was an instructional essay entitled "Hooking is Easy." Mrs. Holden advises:

> In hooking, never use a frame. Besides being passé, they are antisocial, as they cannot be carried about. It is also more restful to hook on the lap and change positions occasionally. Then, too, the finished rug is much more pliant, has a softer effect, and is less "commercial" looking in appearance. When the rug becomes too heavy, it is advisable to place it on a card table or some support. A low slipper chair is ideal for hooking.
>
> The needle is very important. It must be slender, well tapered so as to penetrate burlap readily and not injure fabric.
>
> In cutting material (and we have a cutter that assures uniform widths), the widths vary with texture of fabric, thinner material being cut slightly wider – 3/8" wide is proper size as too small strips are advisable only as hangings or anything that does not receive hard usage.
>
> Hold material in left hand and catch hold of burlap for support; pull material through to the right side to about 1/4" in height. Care should be taken not to pull loops too high or too low. The strips should be pulled through to the right side when beginning and ending. Never cross material underneath.
>
> Start in the center of rug and work out. In geometric designs, work all the flowers first, then fill in the background. Always work pattern first, then scrolls, background and border last.
>
> In working background and border never follow around designs on scrolls or work with weave of burlap either. Begin in the center and work out in any figures you choose and fill in around these. This is called striating; using several shades, and it is more interesting to striate background and borders as it softens their appearance. Our ancestors of course used this method due to lack of materials, but it is still the best method from an artistic standpoint as well as its economical features.
>
> Be sure to sew tape on before beginning border. Sew to the right side and when hooking is finished, whip tape back, leaving a roll on edge so burlap is never exposed. This is why we try to match tape with color of border used.
>
> Never turn back burlap and hook through double as your burlap is exposed and one thread injured, your rug will soon be beyond repair.

Mrs. Holden's recipe for hooking success.

The following pages were reproduced from *Old South Hooked Rug Patterns*.

LOUISIANA STATE EXHIBIT BUILDING
STATE RESOURCE EXHIBITS · STATE ART GALLERY · STATE HISTORICAL MUSEUM
3015 GREENWOOD ROAD
SHREVEPORT, LOUISIANA

June 12, 1947

Mrs. Frank C. Holden
1739 Fairfield Ave.
Shreveport, La.

Dear Mrs. Holden:

Since the exhibit of your hooked rugs last year, I have been much interested in the possibilities of sound design and color harmony in hooked rugs.

Your work shown here at the State Exhibit Building was of a very superior quality in the basic principles which constitute good art in any medium.

Your rugs were truly a delight to all.

Sincerely yours,
H. B. Wright
H.B. Wright, Curator

UNDER THE SUPERVISION OF THE LOUISIANA DEPARTMENT OF AGRICULTURE AND IMMIGRATION · BATON ROUGE, LA.
HARRY D. WILSON, COMMISSIONER · W. E. ANDERSON, ENTOMOLOGIST

A 1947 letter praising Mrs. Holden's design and hooking talents.

Creating a Masterpiece

In making a hooked rug, the pattern or composition is of first importance. In olden times our grandmothers drew their own designs because few were professionally created then. Although we love and prize these old rugs, we must admit the composition of the 20th Century rug is far ahead of them as the aeroplane is the covered wagon.

Hook rug designing is an art. It requires special training or special talent and is most successful when the two are combined.

A good composition must have the right perspective and proper balance, coupled with harmony in color arrangement. Most designs shown herein and listed in supplement are original, the designer of which began studying art at the age of five and who understands composition, balance, color and expression.

Next in importance to design is the foundation or burlap, the bone and sinew of the rug. It must be tested for strength, strongly woven without flaws or weak strands, if it is to be of lasting service. There can be no wide divergence of opinion as to the quality of the material on which the design is drawn. Cheap patterns should never be used as a hooked rug represents much patient labor and to make them of poor composition with improperly dyed and weak materials is indeed "love's labor lost."

The stamping fluid used on pattern must be fast and instant drying in order not to rub off and discolor materials used. If the stamping fluid bleeds or rubs off onto your materials, your finished rug is ruined.

Next consider the color scheme. The rugger should plan the color scheme before beginning the design in order that all will balance and harmonize. It is also very important to use fast Perfection dyes or materials of fast colors.

We must not only have good composition or pattern and fast dyes, but materials which will stand long usage. The material should be clean and strong. Old worn out blankets and clothes which have been weakened by perspiration and cleaning, fray quickly. When purchasing a ready made rug, be sure to ascertain if the materials used are new.

Thus in creating a masterpiece we must have a good composition, strong basic fabric, best quality of woolen materials, properly dyed as to colors and fastness, exquisite shading and fine hooking.

Louisiana Iris

Native Iris in center scroll border 36" x 40", Oval. Designed and made by Mrs. Francis C. Holden.

Bride's Bouquet

Pastel flowers on light background. Beautifully executed. Made by Mrs. A. M. Rizzo, Monroe, La. Designed by Mrs. Francis Holden. 40" x 72".

Shown are examples of finished rugs made from the patterns offered in Mrs. Holden's 1948 catalogue, *Old South Hooked Rug Patterns*. Her patterns were also available at the Colonial Rug Shoppe in Monroe, Louisiana.

La France

One spray taken from unfinished design 48" x 84", containing two large sprays on each end of seven roses and buds with two on sides of five roses and buds. Soft shades, rose and grey green leaves on rose beige background. Exquisite technique and shading, suggestive of needlepoint. Designed and made by Mrs. Francis Holden.

French Scroll

Has interesting rhythm of the scroll in border. Multi-floral center. Designed and made by Mrs. Francis Holden.

Pictured is a work in progress showing the unfinished burlap foundation of "La France" and a completed "French Scroll."

Prize Winner

Laurel Wreath

Very fine in texture, pattern composition and coloring; won first prize in National Rug Show in 1941. Made by Mrs. Francis Holden.

Mrs. Francis Holden was not only a designer; the rugs she hooked won prizes.

Hearth Rug

Reproduced from rug found in Maine. Three-sided design 36" x 67", also 45" x 72". Made by Mrs. H. W. Alleman, Monroe. Unsurpassed in shading, technique and balance.

Keenan

Reproduced from rug made about eighty years ago by relative of former Monroe resident, Mrs. J. F. Keenan, now of Florida. Beautifully executed. Well balanced, exquisite shading and color harmony. Made by Mrs. A. M. Rizzo. Size 36" x 66". Also made in oval.

Two floral designs that are "unsurpassed in shading and well balanced."

LOUISIANA

Prize Winner

Laurel Wreath

Very fine in texture, pattern composition and coloring; won first prize in National Rug Show in 1941. Made by Mrs. Francis Holden.

Twisted Ribbon

Designed and made by Mrs. Francis Holden. Unusual arrangement of flowers and ribbon forming graceful rhythm in border. Size 48" x 84".

Certain rug patterns were offered in a variety of sizes.

New England Floral

Lovely composition showing Aubusson influence, unusual in every detail. Designed and made by Mrs. Francis Holden. 5' x 8', oval, also rectangle.

Petite Scroll

Reproduced from an old museum design found in relative's home, but enlarged. Gorgeous coloring of rose, mauve, tea rose with rich blue scroll. Dubonnet border. Size 36" x 66". Made by Mrs. R. E. Marionneaux.

Kentucky Rose

Beautiful soft shades of rose, greens and blue ribbon on rose beige background. Suggestive of needlepoint. Size 40". Also stamped on 48" burlap. Designed and made by Mrs. Francis Holden.

Splendid examples of Mrs. Holden's design and hooking abilities

Mrs. Holden also offered custom designed hooked rug patterns.

Pictured is the unfinished "Lecie" started by Bernice Holstead Moss (1882-1969) of Vienna and Ruston, Louisiana. "She was my first husband's grandmother. Her daughter, Elizabeth Moss Gilbert gave this rug hooking pattern to me. She said that if you had a dress on that you liked, and if you saw Mother eyeing it, you had better run and hide or she would have your dress in her rug before you knew it." As written on the burlap, "Mrs. F. C. Holden, 1739 Fairfield, Shreveport, Louisiana" designed the pattern "Lecie". Mrs. Francis Holden was a designer for the Colonial Rug Shoppe, in Monroe, Louisiana and her 1948 copyrighted *Old South Hooked Rug Patterns* offers this very same pattern. It is unknown when her move between Shreveport and Monroe took place. The unfinished pattern dates from around 1930s-1940s. *Courtesy of Jane Klinck.*

More words of praise.

HAZEL SARAH EVANS MARSHALL (1897-1989)

Portia Loper recalls her beloved grandmother.

Hazel Marshall always had an "eye for beauty." Born in Amite, Louisiana, in 1897, she always had the prettiest yard, and her daughters and granddaughters were the best dressed because of her love of making beautiful clothes for them. But it wasn't until she was 65 years old that she discovered the joys of creating hand-hooked rugs. She joined an adult education class while living in Santa Cruz, California, and this began her rug hooking adventure. She was a fast hooker. While her classmates were barely getting started on their rugs, Hazel would be finishing hers.

Each one was especially beautiful, hooked in a #2 and #3 cut (2/32", 3/32"). Each one was a work of art; many winning first place prizes at county fairs. Hazel was her happiest when she found white wool army and navy blankets at thrift stores. These wonderful treasures had an almost "cotton" quality and feel to them. She would run home and dye them and cut them for her many rugs.

Hazel passed away in 1989 at the age of 92, but her children and grandchildren fondly remember her "eye for beauty," as they enjoy the wonderful hand-hooked rugs that she left.

A Southerner at heart, it is most appropriate that Hazel Marshall's rugs, pictured below are back at home in Louisiana with her granddaughter, Portia Loper.

A wispy oak leaf wreath frames morning glories, tulips, and roses. Using re-cycled woolen fabrics – army and navy blankets being favorites – Hazel Marshall dyed her thrift store finds, cut the wool into strips 2/32" and 3/32" wide and hooked heirlooms that are now cherished by her Louisiana granddaughter, Portia Loper. Pattern maker unknown. Hooked by Hazel Sarah Evans Marshall. Louisiana and California. 1968. 52" x 33". *Courtesy of Portia P. Loper.*

Fresh from the garden and perhaps reminiscent of her Louisiana flowerbeds, a single rose with foliage and buds was expertly shaded and hooked by Hazel Marshall. Pattern maker unknown. Hooked by Hazel Sarah Evans Marshall. Louisiana and California. 1963. 14" x 11". *Courtesy of Portia P. Loper.*

Another example of Hazel Marshall's creative hand-work. A pastel palette was used to hook "Persian Court." Designed by Pearl McGown. Hooked by Hazel Sarah Evans Marshall. Louisiana and California. 1988. 38" x 72". *Courtesy of Portia P. Loper.*

Portia Loper

Talent runs in the family. Following in her grandmother, Hazel Marshall's footsteps, Portia Loper also enjoys making rugs. She has been hooking for over twenty-five years.

Curving and flowing lines of this Persian-style accent rug were hooked with strips of woolen fabric cut 6/32" wide. The use of earth tones lends an air of antiquity to "Early Persia." Designed by Jane McGown Flynn. House of Price / Charco pattern. Hooked by Portia Loper. Louisiana. 2006. 30" x 44". *Courtesy of Portia P. Loper.*

"Garden's Gift" was hooked under the direction of hooking artist and teacher, Wilma Hill. "As an attempt to shade the flowers accurately, I picked fresh flowers to study but had to keep picking more when they died. Then, I had to wait until the next spring to cut a few more flowers, resulting in a seven-year span of time spent hooking." As was sometimes done in the past when fresh flowers were not available, Portia Loper's special long-term project will eventually "be placed on my coffin, as my grandmother's rug was placed on my mother's coffin." Designed by Jane McGown Flynn. House of Price / Charco pattern. Hooked by Portia Loper. Louisiana. 1996. 46" x 30". *Courtesy of Portia P. Loper.*

An old world Santa, the "Gift Giver" is highlighted by a stippled background and flanked by blooming stars and blue birds of happiness. Patsy Becker pattern. Hooked by Portia Loper. Louisiana. 2007. 42" x 33". *Courtesy of Portia P. Loper.*

"I had been hooking flowers and needed some diversion from formality and realism. 'Hooking Sweet Hooking' provided a needed transition to whimsy and humor. Every new radiant color made me smile! She even sports sequin glasses and toe ring. I dressed her for Christmas and she became my Christmas card." Beverly Conway pattern. Hooked by Portia Loper. Louisiana. 2006. 44" x 36". *Courtesy of Portia P. Loper.*

From the outside looking in, a "Candle's Glow" lights up the face of a frozen friend. Designed by Victoria Hart Ingalls. Hooked by Portia Loper. Louisiana. 2008. 9" x 12". *Courtesy of Portia P. Loper*.

RUG HOOKING IN LOUISIANA TODAY

Over the years interest in rug hooking in the "Pelican State" has steadily increased. Louisiana's hooking artists proudly display their work.

Dorothy Delaune

A lattice work border frames lush "Hydrangeas." Designed by Jane McGown Flynn. House of Price / Charco pattern. Hooked by Dorothy Delaune. Louisiana. 2003. 27" x 43". *Courtesy of Dorothy Delaune*.

"Aunt Jemima," complete with bandana, apron, and grocery list, recalls another era. First associated with ready mix cooking and introduced to the public in 1889, the fictional Southern cook is today a well-recognized logo for several Quaker Oats Company food products. Designed by Sue Waukel. Hooked by Dorothy Delaune. Louisiana. 2007. 44" x 39". *Courtesy of Dorothy Delaune.*

"Primitive Angels," each holding a flag, recalls Southern folk art of long ago. Designed by Sue Hoss. Hooked by Dorothy Delaune, Louisiana. 2002. 32" x 41.5". *Courtesy of Dorothy Delaune.*

Marilyn Connor

Complete with an attached buzzing bee, "Sunflower Purse" makes a green fashion statement. Designed by Carrie Martin and Marilyn Connor. Hooked by Marilyn Connor. Louisiana. 2007. 32" x 9". *Courtesy of Marilyn S. Connor*.

Trimmed in berry red, stylized stones frame a "Winterberry" tree, that provides a welcomed treat for three cardinals. Resembling ice crystals on glass, the impressionistic arched sky adds another dimension of interest to this frosty vignette. Primco pattern. Hooked by Marilyn Connor. Louisiana. 2008. 27" x 23.5". *Courtesy of Marilyn S. Connor.*

As a nursing student, Marilyn Connor rode the New Orleans streetcars to visit friends and relax in the French Quarter. Her "Desire," set against a swirling van Gogh-like sky, honors the 1951 Oscar award winning film. Designed and hooked by Marilyn Connor. Louisiana. 2005. 17" x 31.5". *Courtesy of Marilyn S. Connor.*

June Brockhoeft

"Pomegranate Basket" combines fruit, flower, and foliage with geometric motifs. A hit or miss stripe border echoes the colors used within this hearth-style design. Designed by Susan Quicksall / Holly Hill Design. Hooked by June Brockhoeft. Louisiana. 2008. 21" x 48". *Courtesy of June Brockhoeft.*

Started in February and completed in July, June Brockhoeft's "Button Basket," hooked in pleasing earthy tones, recalls early American needlework. Designed by Susan Quicksall / Holly Hill Design. Hooked by June Brockhoeft. Louisiana. 2008. 32" x 43". *Courtesy of June Brockhoeft.*

Gerri Bischoff

A soft speckled background sets the stage for the jewel-like tones of "Pineapple Antique." Quail Hill Designs pattern. Hooked by Gerri Bischoff. Louisiana. 2007. 24.5" x 48". *Courtesy of Gerri Bischoff.*

Minus the fruit, "Gerri's Sampler" borrows motifs from her aforementioned "Pineapple Antique." Designed and hooked by Gerri Bischoff. Louisiana. 2008. 22" x 36". *Courtesy of Gerri Bischoff.*

Cindy Vaccaro

After her sister saw a rug hooking demonstration at a Louisiana fair, Cindy Vaccaro decided to give the new-found craft a try. At first she hated it. Now she loves it. Trimmed in blue plaid, "Fantasy Garden" sports four blue birds and imaginary flowers. Susan Quicksall / Holly Hill Design. Hooked by Cindy Vaccaro. Louisiana. 2008. 29" x 53.5". *Courtesy of Cindy Vaccaro.*

Bold and fanciful blossoms, set against a contour hooked background, spring forth from a decorative basket. "Old Penn Floral." Susan Quicksall / Holly Hill Design. Hooked by Cindy Vaccaro. Louisiana. 2007. 25" x 37.5". *Courtesy of Cindy Vaccaro.*

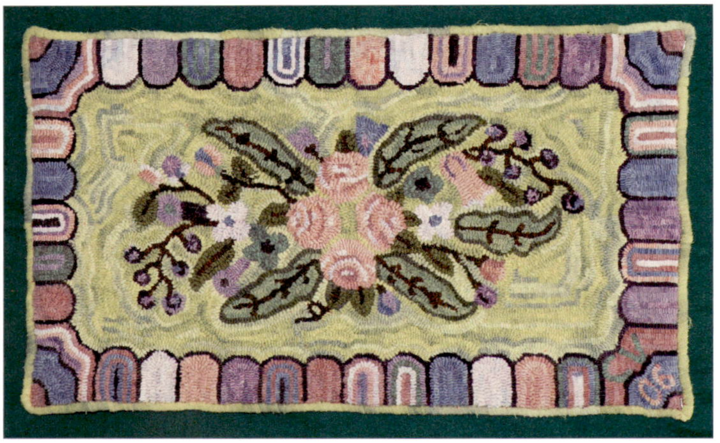

Admiring patterns popular over a century ago, Cindy Vacarro chose a springtime palette and hooked her first rug. A lamb's tongue border contains the floral center. Designed and hooked by Cindy Vaccaro. Louisiana. 2006. 20" x 33". *Courtesy of Cindy Vacarro*.

Far left:
A simple "Columbia County Carnation" worked up in blue, framed and ready to hang. Designed by Susan Feller / Ruckman Mill Farm. Hooked by Cindy Vaccaro. Louisiana. 2008. 11.5" x 9". *Courtesy of Cindy Vaccaro.*

Left:
Shoot a gun through the front door and the bullets will fly out the back door. This New Orleans home is decked out and ready for visitors – gun toting and otherwise. "N. O. Shotgun." Designed by Diane Stoffel. Hooked by Cindy Vacarro. Louisiana. 2008. 15.5" x 13.5". *Courtesy of Cindy Vacarro.*

Ada Brinsko

Fun to hook; fun to look at. This age defying "Geometric" rug would add a decorative touch to any room setting. Designed by Carrie Martin. Hooked by Ada Brinsko. Louisiana. 2008. 36" x 54". *Courtesy of Ada T. Brinsko.*

A favorite pattern of rug hookers throughout the United States, "Sail Cloth" was Ada Brinsko's first rug hooking project. Shades of red and blue make for a lively design. Heirloom Rugs pattern. Hooked by Ada Brinsko. Louisiana. 2007. 21" x 42". *Courtesy of Ada T. Brinsko.*

Carrie Martin

A native of California, Carrie Martin brought her collection of antique rugs to Louisiana and decided to learn how to hook. The rest is history. She has been teaching rug hooking for over 20 years. Pictured is her version of the popular "Sail Cloth" pattern. Heirloom Rugs pattern. Hooked by Carrie Martin. Louisiana. 2005. 23.5" x 54." *Courtesy of Carrie Martin.*

"Kitchen Rug" is a cheerful hooked sampler meant to brighten your day and make your morning cup of coffee more enjoyable. Designed and hooked by Carrie Martin. Louisiana. 2005. 29" x 38". *Courtesy of Carrie Martin.*

Barbara Reilly

The surrounding landscape may be stark but the four columned "Pink House" boasts shrubs in full bloom, a lit front porch, and tapestry-like drapes in the windows. Awarding herself the prize for the longest time to finish a rug, Barbara Reilly first drew her pattern in 1983, started hooking 1984, and finally completed the hooked house project in 2007. Adapted from a pen and ink sketch. Designed and hooked by Barbara Reilly. Louisiana. 2007. 26" x 36". *Courtesy of Barbara Reilly.*

A unique coupling of colors makes for an aesthetically pleasing "Early Persia." Note the plaid binding around the rug's outer edge echoes the colors within. Designed by Jane McGown Flynn. House of Price / Charco pattern. Hooked by Barbara Reilly. Louisiana. 2007. 30" x 44". *Courtesy of Barbara Reilly.*

WILMA HILL

Baton Rouge, Louisiana

In the 1930s commercially made carpet was readily available and inexpensive to buy. There was no need to hook your own rugs and the interest in the craft was waning. Instrumental in a spirited revival in the hooking tradition was Massachusetts-born Pearl McGown (1892-1983). Recognized as a designer of exquisite patterns, instructor of hooking teachers nationwide, and the author of four books on the craft, Pearl McGown gained notoriety as the "Grande Dame" of rug hooking.

Inheriting her late grandmother's love of hooked rugs and artistic abilities, Jane McGown Flynn designs a popular line of hooking patterns for House of Price / Charco Patterns of Mars, Pennsylvania.

Today, throughout The Deep South, as well as world-wide, the McGown standard of excellence among rug hooking teachers remains strong. A popular and sought after hooking instructor, Wilma Hill is a certified McGown teacher.

I learned rug hooking in the early 1970s from Phyllis Regan, a wonderful McGown teacher in Chattanooga. Phyllis, along with Ramona Maddox, was responsible for starting the popular Castle in the Clouds Rug Hooking School held annually on Lookout Mountain in Georgia.

In 1974 my family moved from Chattanooga, with its very active group of rug hookers, to Baton Rouge, Louisiana, where there were none. For several years I hooked alone, phoning Phyllis when I ran into problems I couldn't solve. Eventually she persuaded me to attend a McGown Teachers' Workshop in Jekyll Island, Georgia, as a trainee. Unfortunately Phyllis died before I received my certification in 1984.

I opened a studio in my home in 1985, and began teaching rug classes. In 1993, a group of my students became the Baton Rouge Rugger Roux Chapter of the National McGown Association. This group presented many shows and demonstrations in the Baton Rouge area, and in 1998 sponsored the Plantation Rug Hooking Workshop at Tezcuco, a beautiful antebellum plantation setting located on the Mississippi River just southeast of the city. I served as director of this workshop for seven years before retiring to move to Arkansas in 2006. During the years in Baton Rouge I taught well over 200 students in the studio, as well as classes at teachers' workshops.

Rug hooking has been a great joy to me for a good number of years, and I have completed over a hundred pieces in a variety of styles and patterns. I learned to hook from a teacher who was an expert in hooking and shading with a narrow cut, and while I have enjoyed teaching and experimenting with wide cut, prodding, felting, alternative materials, etc., the challenge of creating a realistic effect with a fine cut is still my first love. I am proud of the hundreds of pieces that have been done by my students, and keep picture albums of their work in my files. I only hope that they have learned as much from me as I have learned from them through the years!

"'The devil is in the details' is a saying we often hear. But for me it should be the challenge in the details. 'American Homestead – Winter' was my first pictorial attempt, and it was truly a bit of a challenge. There are lots of different scraps, all cut in a #3 cut (3/32" wide strips of woolen fabric) except for some of the tiny lines in the shutters, chimneys, and decorative details that were often done with a single thread. A lot of brown and gray plaids were used in the trees, and I dyed the colors for the sky and snow. Wonderful fun!" Designed by Jane McGown Flynn. House of Price / Charco pattern. Hooked by Wilma Hill. Louisiana. 1982. 26" x 40". *Courtesy of Wilma Hill.*

"Naomi Stopher, a McGown teacher who is now deceased, selected the colors for 'Oriental Hen.' I had my doubts about the apricot background, but it proved to be the ideal shade to set off the deep, rich colors of the hen." Designed by Jane McGown Flynn. House of Price / Charco pattern. Hooked by Wilma Hill. Louisiana. 1986. 27" x 21". *Courtesy of Wilma Hill*

"'Freedom' has quite a history. It was started many, many years ago by a woman who was unable to complete it. I would guess that about one third of it was done when I bought it at a teacher's workshop auction. My husband is a duck hunter, and I knew he would like this piece for his den wall. There was quite a bit of the original hooking wool included in the package, but definitely not enough to complete the project. The first problem was to try to match the colors that the first hooker had used, complicated by the fact that the work was so old that the hooked colors had begun to fade a bit from their original shades. Then there was the problem of technique – the style of hooking the sky, water, and trees was already established, and trying to imitate that style was one of the most difficult things I have ever tried. The burlap was also unstable, and several patches had to be made in both the older portion as well as the unhooked part. All of this aside, the finished result is a treasured piece that my husband absolutely refuses to let me remove from the wall for a show or exhibit or any other reason." Pearl McGown pattern. Hooked by Wilma Hill. Louisiana. 1988. 26" x 46". *Courtesy of Wilma Hill.*

"When I selected 'Coral Reef,' I dyed some of the colors with Rit neon dyes, and found them to be much like the actual bright colors of tropical fish. When the fish were hooked, there remained the problem of a watery background. After a little experimenting, I used an opalescent rope twist of plastic that is ordinarily used for bows in floral arranging. After I opened the twist, I cut it into strips like the wool, and hooked it as usual. The result is a watery, shimmery background that complements the colorful fish. I did not know how the plastic would retain its shine over the years, but the picture hung for fifteen years in a bathroom that had no ventilation, and in which my children took the longest, steamiest showers possible. The picture looks exactly the same as it did when it was first done." Designed by Jane McGown Flynn. House of Price / Charco pattern. Hooked by Wilma Hill. Louisiana. 1988. 20" x 32". *Courtesy of Wilma Hill.*

"I was standing in the Dorr Mill Store in Guild, New Hampshire one summer, and the 'Twelve Days of Christmas' pattern had just come by mail to the store. I must have taught this song to two thousand children over the years, and I knew I had to do the pattern. It was fun from the first loop – no repetition, and a chance to use lots of scraps. Now, whenever I can't remember how many swans were swimming or how many pipers were piping, I can just check the rug!" Jacqueline Hansen Designs. Hooked by Wilma Hill. Louisiana. 1990. 26" x 38". *Courtesy of Wilma Hill.*

"I found this adorable 'Frog A Wooing' pattern in Kennebunkport, Maine – it was designed by Joan Moshimer. Of the hundreds of pieces I have hooked over the years, I think this is my favorite. He is just so handsome and dapper, and has such a happy, froggy look. How could Miss Mousie turn him down?" W. Cushing and Company pattern. Hooked by Wilma Hill. Louisiana. 1994. 48" x 32". *Courtesy of Wilma Hill.*

"When I had the opportunity to hook with Victoria Ingalls of Independence, Missouri, I selected 'Bear Portrait' as my project. Victoria's superior sense of color and shading made the effort a totally delightful experience, and the stories she told about each bear in the portrait gave a new meaning to the work." Victoria Hart Ingalls pattern. Hooked by Wilma Hill. Louisiana. 2005. 36" x 48". *Courtesy of Wilma Hill.*

Louisiana State University Tiger Rug

The mascot for LSU's proud and highly competitive athletic teams is the tiger. The "Tigers" nickname and logo was chosen to honor two Louisiana brigades that fought so fiercely during the Civil War they became known as the "Louisiana Tigers." In 1924, the university received its first live mascot, "Little-Eat-'Em-Up" from an alumnus in South America. Unfortunately the giant cat was retired after the end of the football season due to "failure to act."

Today spirit remains strong. Get in the way of the fighting faithful and you'll be "tiger bait."

Hooking artist Wilma Hill recalls the story of her "LSU Tiger" hooked rug.

With hook in hand, Wilma Hill poses with her "LSU Tiger" rug. 2008. *Courtesy of Wilma Hill.*

> When Huey P. Long was the governor of Louisiana from 1928 until 1932, he began some extensive renovations to the LSU campus. The projects often featured various works of art in the form of murals, friezes, and mosaics. The completion of what is now the Huey P. Long Field House included a seven-foot round floor mosaic of a tiger's head, surrounded by a Latin inscription and colorful geometric border. For 30 years my husband taught in the Department of Kinesiology, which is now housed in the Field House. Every day he walked across the mosaic, and we often remarked about the artistic talent of the person who created the work, and about how well its rich earthy colors would look hooked into a rug using the original as a pattern. The challenge became a dare, and one year when the students were away for Mardi Gras holiday we traced the pattern and transferred it to a monk's cloth backing. I collected wool in many colors of the tiger, and began hooking the expressive face. As I worked to duplicate the different sections of the design, I gained a great appreciation for the awesome skill of the artist. The tile chips were not all square, as is often the case in mosaic work, but had been painstakingly cut and honed to make features such as the pointed whiskers and fangs, round teeth, and shaggy sections of the fur surrounding the animal's head.
>
> At first I considered hooking only the tiger in the center of the piece, but I soon realized that neither the stark black and white band containing the inscription, nor the bright wavy pattern of the outside border could be eliminated without diminishing the impressive overall effect of the original pattern.
>
> As I progressed with hooking the piece, I began to try to find information about the designer, not only to give credit for the extraordinary work, but to satisfy my own curiosity about the person who was capable of producing such artistry. Through the years I have researched countless sources in the LSU archives, as well as libraries, the Internet, and personal interviews, but regret to report that so far I have been unable to find even the slightest clue to the identity. Possibly the most accurate theory came from Katherine Long, ex-wife of Senator Russell Long, who is now deceased. She was of the opinion that the person had been a WPA artist, one of the many who traveled about the country in the 1930s producing such creations and often remaining

anonymous. I continue to hope that at some point there will be information about the artist, but it may not exist.

Now living in Arkansas, Wilma Hill loaned her hooked "LSU Tiger" rug to the Foundation for Historical Louisiana for its 2008 fundraising campaign. It was placed in the Huey Long bedroom of the old Governor's Mansion in Baton Rouge. The mansion is now a museum. A local television station filmed the unveiling of the rug and made note that the "LSU Tiger" rug was a work in progress for 27 years, and has approximately 750,000 loops. To the delight of Wilma Hill, the evening news special feature ended with a closing commentary by the commentator saying that this was "one art form saluting another."

Photos of Wilma Hill and the "LSU Tiger" rug are courtesy of Mr. John's Photography, Fort Smith, Arkansas.

Wilma Hill's "LSU Tiger" rug is a hooked copy of a tile mosaic inlayed into the floor of the Louisiana State University Field House. Original designer of the mosaic is unknown. Hooked by Wilma Hill. Arkansas. 2008. Diameter 7'. *Courtesy of Wilma Hill.*

Rug hooking teacher Wilma Hill shares the story of Tezcuco Plantation Home, and her friend and student, Annette Harland.

Plantations have long been a part of Southern culture, and many are located along the Mississippi River in Louisiana. One especially lovely plantation was called Tezcuco, a name meaning "resting place" in the Indian language. Located a few miles outside of Baton Rouge, Tezcuco, (built in 1855) was a bed and breakfast facility featuring authentic and unique Cajun cottages for guests that were charmingly furnished with antiques from the Civil War era. The large plantation home was an excellent example of the antebellum style of most plantations, and was toured by thousands of visitors each year. One of the area's finest restaurants was located on the property, serving the best of Louisiana's cuisine in a cozy rustic setting. The small chapel on the property was the setting for many formal weddings and celebrations, and the large green lawns leading to the levee of the Mississippi held magnificent ancient live oaks draped with strands of hanging moss. This was the perfect place for dancing and outdoor receptions. Many of the other features, too numerous to mention, made Tezcuco a priority for those who wanted a taste of life as it would have been during the days of the great plantations.

Annette Harland, a Michigan native, moved to Louisiana in the 1990s, and purchased the Tezcuco property. Her excellent skills in the art of gracious Southern hospitality turned the plantation into one of the most popular tourist attractions in the state.

Annette discovered the Baton Rouge rug hookers at a demonstration on another local plantation, Magnolia Mound. She was very interested in the work being done, and soon became a student of the art. From the first loop, it was clear that Annette had an unusual talent for rug hooking, and her greatest wish was to be able to hook a picture of her plantation to frame and hang in her home. Ignoring all cautions about the enormity of such a project as a beginning hooker, she was determined to accomplish this wish. She developed her own pattern from a small picture of the home, and soon she was ready to start the actual hooking. Before long, she had completed a lovely picture of Tezcuco.

Annette Harland moved to Louisiana in 1994 where she purchased and lovingly restored and operated The Tezcuco Plantation Home, a charming bed and breakfast located on the Mississippi River, a few miles outside of Baton Rouge. The large plantation was an excellent example of the antebellum style and housed antiques from the Civil War era. Pictured are two views of the Louisiana landmark, which sadly was destroyed by fire in 2002. Photos taken in 2000. *Courtesy of Annette Harland.*

In 1998, Annette graciously offered her beautiful plantation for the first Plantation Rug Hooking Workshop. The unique setting, friendly staff, hard-working local ruggers, and the excellent teachers attracted a large group of students, and the 60-guest capacity of the bed and breakfast was soon filled. For four wonderful years, Tezcuco provided a perfect location for this popular workshop, and participants were eagerly looking forward to the fifth one to be held in February 2003. Tragically this never happened because on Mother's Day of 2002, a devastating fire destroyed the legendary Tezcuco Plantation Home. Luckily the beautiful picture that Annette Harland had hooked was located in her private home and therefore saved. Although Annette was forced to close the plantation and move back to Michigan, she spends several months in Baton Rouge enjoying the culture and friends that she loved as an "honorary Southerner."

Sadly Annette Harland passed away in May of 2010. Her obituary in Michigan's *Traverse City Record-Eagle* read in part, "Annette was blessed by a loving family and friends. She enjoyed various social outlets including travel, The Red Hats, and numerous rug hooking groups. Her countless wool strip hooked rugs were works of art, and although Annette took her talent very seriously, she loved to joke that she was an experienced 'hooker.'"

Annette Harland's first hooking project was her beloved Louisiana estate. Fortunately her hooked likeness of "Tezcuco Home Plantation" was safely stored at another location at the time of the devastating fire that destroyed the landmark in 2002. Designed and hooked by Annette Harland. Louisiana. 1998. 37" x 53". *Courtesy of Annette Harland.*

Chapter 3

MISSISSIPPI: The "Magnolia State"

The Great Mississippi, the majestic,
the magnificent Mississippi;
rolling its mile-wide tide along,
shining in the sun.
—Mark Twain

Birthplace of the blues and Elvis Presley, the "Magnolia State" is known for its good Southern cooking and gracious living. Claiming sites of some of the fiercest battles of the Civil War, Mississippi also witnessed the defining moments of the American Civil Rights Movement. Given the Ojibwa name meaning "Great River," this Deep South state was, and is, deeply affected by "Old Man River" — the Mighty Mississippi. Riverboats and historical homes share a lush landscape; attracting those that choose a more relaxed and gentler way of life.

All photos in this chapter, with the exception of the Oxford Rug Camp, are courtesy of Marcus McClamrock / Shade Tree Graphics, Brandon, Mississippi.

Seaside and resting comfortably, a colorful "Catfish" brings a smile to all. A delightful work in progress. Adapted from M. Shaw Folk Art by Spruce Ridge Studios. Hooked by Cindy Mansel. Mississippi. 2008. 19" x 46". *Courtesy of Cindy Mansel.*

Laverette Buford Poole

Cynthia Poole Barlow recalls her family's rug hooking history:

> These rugs were hooked by my grandmother, Laverette Buford Poole, in the late 1950s to early 1960s. She made her rugs from World War II blankets, our woolen coats, and any other wool material that she could recycle. I have fond memories of sitting at her card table shredding the wool and dyeing the fabric beautiful colors on her stove. She enjoyed rug hooking until her eyesight failed. She made rugs for her two children and for each of her grandchildren. She lived her later years with my parents. I remember how embarrassed my parents were when she was introduced to the new pastor in town and she said, "I bet you didn't know that I used to be a hooker!"

This family photo, taken in Jackson, Mississippi, during the 1950s, shows a seated Leigh Ann Buford surrounded by her four daughters. From left to right are: Laura Lynnell Buford Rochester, Byrdie Buford Long, Laverette Buford Poole and Bea Buford Quinn. Pictured are rugs hooked by sisters Laverette and Laura Lynnell. These rugs have been passed down to Cynthia Poole Barlow and Judy Rochester Fain, granddaughters of the two sisters. Honoring the family tradition, the Mississippi cousins, Cynthia and Judy, enjoy hooking rugs just as their grandmothers did decades ago. *Courtesy of Judy Rochester Fain.*

Exquisitely hooked; "Magnolias" are a fixture in the South representing beauty, perseverance, and dignity. It is also the state flower of Mississippi. Pattern maker unknown. Hooked by Laverette Buford Poole. Mississippi. Early 1960s. 34.5" x 17". *Courtesy of Cynthia Poole Barlow.*

Mrs. Poole was born in 1894 and died in 1998, at the age of 104. She lived most of her life in Monticello, Mississippi.

Rose bud and foliage swags complement a central "Pretty Posey" floral motif. Note the scalloped interior field. Designed by Medora H. Kitchens, Paragould, Arkansas. Hooked by Laverette Buford Poole. Mississippi. 1957. 55" x 36". *Courtesy of Cynthia Poole Barlow.*

A bouquet of stylized flowers, placed on a scalloped gray field, is framed by a black border. Lacking the sophistication of her aforementioned rugs, perhaps this is an early attempt at rug hooking. Hooked by Laverette Buford Poole. Mississippi. 1950s. 40.5" x 31". *Courtesy of Cynthia Poole Barlow.*

Delicate bunches of pastel "Violets" form an oval wreath hooked especially for granddaughter, Cynthia. A single flower and a trio of leaves make for a dainty corner detail. Pattern maker unknown. Hooked by Laverette Buford Poole. Mississippi. 1950s. 64" x 36". *Courtesy of Cynthia Poole Barlow.*

"Oak Leaves and Acorns" frame a simple diamond grid. Pattern maker unknown. Hooked by Laverette Buford Poole. Mississippi. Late 1950s. 54" x 35". *Courtesy of Cynthia Poole Barlow.*

Laura Lynnell Buford Rochester

Two red roses, complete with buds and foliage, are the focal point of this oval rug. A decorative tray-like design separates the inner and outer fields. Pattern from Herrschners catalog. Hooked by Laura Lynnell Buford Rochester. Mississippi. 1950s. 44" x 23". *Courtesy of Judy Rochester Fain.*

Sharing woolen fabrics and the joys of rug hooking, Laura Lynnell Buford Rochester, younger sister of the aforementioned Laverette Buford Poole, hooked her own version of "Oak Leaves and Acorns." Mrs. Rochester was born in 1898 and died in 1971. Her hooked rug is a now in the possession of her granddaughter, Jane Rochester Fain also of Mississippi. Pattern maker unknown. Hooked by Laura Lynnell Buford Rochester. 1950s. Mississippi. 53" x 34.5". *Courtesy of Judy Rochester Fain*.

Winnie Pearl Taylor Nored

A beautiful unfinished hooked rug from the past.

Pictured is a portion of a unfinished rug hooked by Winnie Pearl Taylor Nored (1919-1991) who was born and raised in Duck Hill, Mississippi. She spent 40 years of her married life living in Greenwood, Mississippi where she owned and operated the Mary-Win Knit Shop during the 1960s. Pattern maker unknown. 1940s-1960s. *Courtesy of JoLynn Vaughn.*

MISSISSIPPI RUG HOOKING TODAY

Feast your eyes on what is being hooked in Mississippi today.

Carolyn Campbell

Fruit, fashion, and a flair for the whimsical, Carolyn Campbell's "Watermelon Clutch" is a charming bit of functional hooking humor. "I remember my great Aunt Maude hooking a rug when I was a young girl. It was a floral design with a black background. It made quite an impression on my young mind." Designed by Jacque Juvenal. Hooked by Carolyn Campbell. Mississippi. 2008. 6" x 12". *Courtesy of Carolyn Campbell.*

It's hare heaven for these "Bunnies in the Garden," an abundance of fruit and flowers delight the devilish duo. Hooked with woolen yarns. Claire Murray Design. Hooked by Carolyn Campbell. Mississippi. 1993. 27" x 33". *Courtesy of Carolyn Campbell.*

Thirty two circles; no two alike. "Circles and Stars" was hooked with a combination of woolen yarns and fabrics. Designed by Lisanne Miller. Hooked by Cynthia Campbell. Mississippi. 2007. 14.5" x 27.5". *Courtesy of Carolyn Campbell.*

Bonnie Curtis

"I started hooking with a group of great friends in Oxford, Mississippi. We meet once a month. We have the best time creating heirlooms for our children." What child aged six to sixty wouldn't love "Garden Hare." A wily, blue-eyed bunny rides the wind while tangled up in a free flowing vine. Designed by Charles Gay. Hooked by Bonnie Curtis. Mississippi. 2005. 28" x 44". *Courtesy of Bonnie Curtis.*

Lost after dark? Perhaps the tiny legs of this robust wandering ewe failed to carry her home before nightfall. A trio of stars lights the way for "Woolley Sheep." Note the curve in the cheerful block border mimics the wave of her thick coat. Designed by Barbara Carroll – Woolley Fox pattern. Hooked by Bonnie Curtis. Mississippi. 2003. 27" x 35". *Courtesy of Bonnie Curtis.*

Lisanne Miller

Offering rug hooking instruction, supplies, and a most pleasant social setting, Lisanne Miller's "P is for Primitive" attracts hooking and fiber artists from near and far. Located in picturesque Canton, Mississippi, the shop also carries knitting and punch hook equipment, specialty foods and an ever-changing array of antiques and collectibles. 2008. *Courtesy of P is for Primitive.*

Six "petal-like" sections are hooked then sewn together creating a squat "Primitive Pumpkin." The variegated skin is hooked from "oodles of wool noodles" in oranges, greens, and browns. An old tree limb forms the stem. Designed and hooked by Lisanne Miller. Mississippi. 2008. 11.5" x 13". *Courtesy of Lisanne Miller*.

A red wind-swept background, hooked from nine different plaids, highlights this "Primitive Pony" weathervane and ribbon banner. Designed and hooked by Lisanne Miller. Mississippi. 2007. 22.5" x 28.5". *Courtesy of Lisanne Miller*.

"'Patriotic Parade' was a pleasure to hook until it came time to do the background. Finally after much thought 'purple mountains majesty' came to mind." Add some ribbon details in the border and you have fireworks. Uncle Sam leads an assorted trio of red, white, and blue clad friends. Designed and hooked by Lisanne Miller. Mississippi. 2006. 22" x 46". *Courtesy of Lisanne Miller.*

A drawing done on planking and found in Maine inspired "Barn Floor Floral." To create the "look of an old rug," a palette of "neutral" woolen fabrics was used. Designed and hooked by Lisanne Miller. Mississippi. 2007. 22.5" x 35". *Courtesy of Lisanne Miller.*

Hand-dyed woolen fabrics were used to hook "Reservoir Herons." "I was inspired by all the wonderful herons that I see daily on the nearby Ross Barnett Reservoir." Designed and hooked by Lisanne Miller. Mississippi. 2008. 21" x 30". *Courtesy of Lisanne Miller.*

Pictured is "My First Rug." A wreath of carrots and running hares capture a simple cookie cutter-like bunny. Designed and hooked by Lisanne Miller. Mississippi. 1994. 27" x 40". *Courtesy of Lisanne Miller.*

"Paisley Purse," hooked with hand-dyed materials as well as mohair, chenille, and strips of suede, "is fantastic because I used up scraps of woolen yarn and fabrics and hooked with upbeat colors." Designed and hooked by Lisanne Miller. Mississippi. 2008. 11" x 8.5". *Courtesy of Lisanne Miller*.

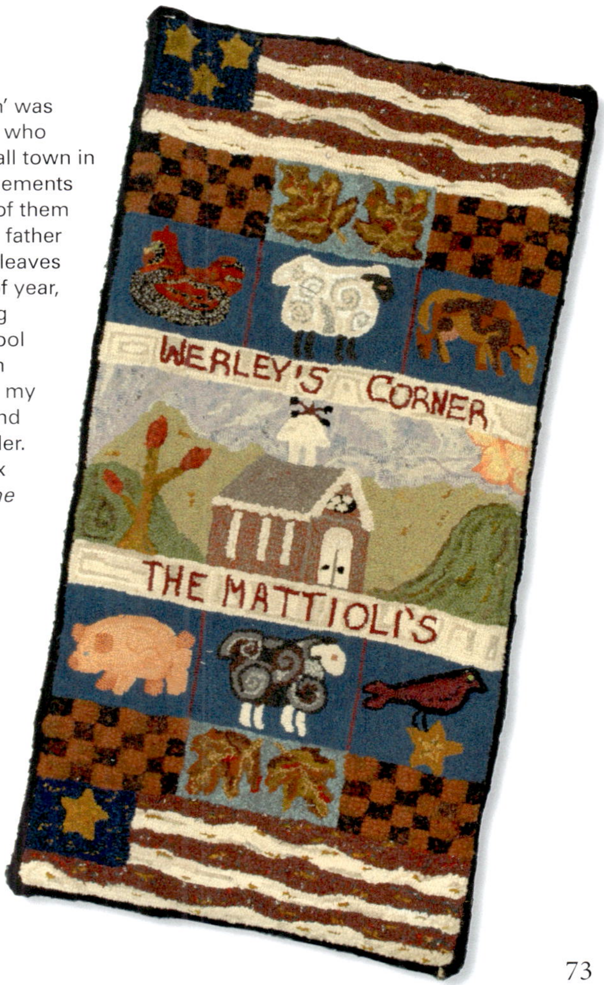

"'Mattioli Family Album' was hooked for my parents who 'finally' retired to a small town in Pennsylvania. All the elements of the rug depict both of them – the flags because my father is a retired Marine, fall leaves for their favorite time of year, animals on neighboring farms, and the old school building that was down the street; a favorite of my mother's." Designed and hooked by Lisanne Miller. Mississippi. 2005. 37" x 24". *Courtesy of Lisanne Miller*.

Barbara Riley

A Texas rug hooker in the Mississippi chapter? No… the author did not make a mistake. Barbara Riley may call the "Lone Star State" home, but she often travels to Canton, Mississippi, to hook with members of The Magnolia Wool Dust Society.

"I've been hooking for about a year and a half and can't stop." Barbara Riley lives in Texas but travels to Canton, Mississippi to take hooking lessons at Lisanne Miller's shop, "P is for Primitive." "Folk Art Star" shines for all who view it and has led Barbara to rug hooking in the Deep South. Designed by Monika Jones. Hooked by Barbara Riley. Texas. 2008. Diameter 40". *Courtesy of Barbara Riley.*

Always a popular pattern, this "Hit or Miss Cabin," is a favorite of both quilters and rug hookers. Designed by Sherry White. Hooked by Barbara Riley. Texas. 2008. 32" x 42". *Courtesy of Barbara Riley.*

A lively striped background was used to highlight "1808 Weathervane Horse." The outer block border reminds one of sun shining through a stained glass window. Adapted from a pattern designed by Paula Alders. Hooked by Barbara Riley. Texas. 2008. 29.5" x 31". *Courtesy of Barbara Riley.*

Cindy Mansel

Seaside and resting comfortably, a colorful "Catfish" brings a smile to all. A delightful work in progress. Adapted from M. Shaw Folk Art by Spruce Ridge Studios. Hooked by Cindy Mansel. Mississippi. 2008. 19" x 46". *Courtesy of Cindy Mansel.*

Rug hookers are a patriotic lot. And proudly raise their hooks to "Freedom." Pattern maker unknown. Hooked by Cindy Mansel. Mississippi. 2003.16" x 32". *Courtesy of Cindy Mansel*

Churchill McKinney

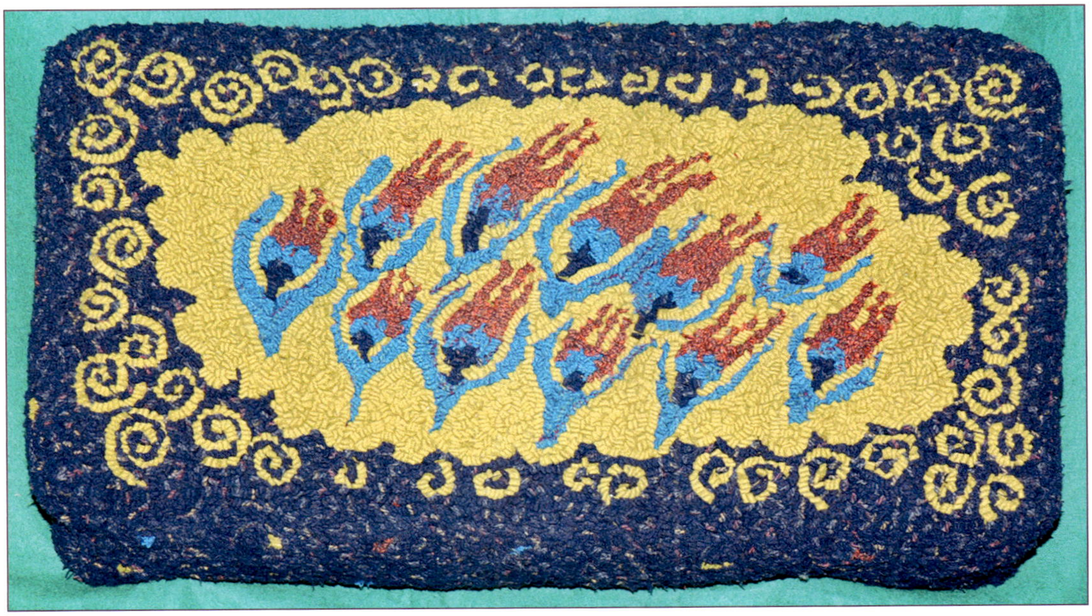

While sitting on her porch, Churchill McKinney felt the need to raise her feet a bit. So she had a wooden stool made, hooked a cover for it, and has been comfortable ever since. This "Flower Tile" motif was adapted from a photo of a Turkish tile and made into a pattern for "this very special lady" by Lisanne Miller. Hooked by Churchill McKinney. Mississippi. 2007. 14" x 28". *Courtesy of Churchill McKinney*.

The fence that surrounds the Church of All Nations on the Mount of Olives in Jerusalem is quite unusual and was the motivation behind Churchill McKinney's hooked "Gate Rug." The church, designed by Antonio Barluzzi, was under construction from 1919 to 1924 using funds from twelve different countries, thus the name. It was built on the traditional site of the Garden of Gethsemane and symbols relating to Biblical stories are depicted throughout the church itself. However, there is little to no information concerning the symbols depicted on the gate. Working from a photograph Lisanne Miller designed the pattern. Hooked by Churchill McKinney. Mississippi. 2007. 29" x 42". *Courtesy of Churchill McKinney.*

A work in progress. "Daghestan Prayer." New Earth Designs. Hooked by Churchill McKinney. Mississippi. 2008. 40" x 62". *Courtesy of Churchill McKinney.*

Ernestine O'Reilly Young

"'Potted Floral' was fun to hook because of the different types of wool used and it was the first large hooking project I attempted." A squat pot holds fantasy flowers. Designed by Lisanne Miller. Hooked by Ernestine O'Reilly Young. Mississippi. 2008. 32" x 40". *Courtesy of Ernestine O'Reilly Young.*

Rug hookers are into re-cycling and "Scrappy Circles" uses left over woolen fabrics in a most charming way. Designed by Lisanne Miller. Hooked by Frances Dunaway. Mississippi. 2008. 21" x 30". *Courtesy of Frances Dunaway.*

A snowflake border frames "Santa and Friends" as the jolly old man prepares for his nighttime flight. Designed by Judy Criss. Hooked by Frances Dunaway. Mississippi. 2007. 43.5" x 25.5". *Courtesy of Frances Dunaway.*

Devastation caused by the forces of nature affect all… including hard hit Gulf Coast rug hookers. Picking up her strength, a hook, and the woolen fabrics donated to her hooking group after Hurricane Katrina, Frances Dunaway created a rug. After adapting a design she admired in *Quilting the Garden*, she made a stencil, applied the pattern to rug hooking linen and went to work. Her fantasy flowers float above a decorative container joining a quintet of stars. Adapted from *Quilting the Garden* by Barb Adams and Alma Allen. Hooked by Frances Dunaway. Mississippi. 2008. 20.5" x 28". *Courtesy of Frances Dunaway.*

"Paisley Pumpkin," complete with paisley hooked ribs, evokes thoughts of a bountiful autumn harvest. Designed by Anita White. Hooked by Frances Dunaway. Mississippi. 2006. 8" x 8". *Courtesy of Frances Dunaway.*

JAIL HOUSE ROCK
Canton, Mississippi

Elvis may have left the building but the rug hookers haven't. Twice a year members of The Magnolia Wool Dust Society, a chapter of ATHA (Association of Traditional Hooking Artists), bring their hooks, their wools, and their rugs to the restored and air-conditioned, historic Madison Jail in Canton, Mississippi. "Join The Magnolia Wool Dust Society for one or two days of creative fun and fellowship with hourly door prizes, great goody bags, wonderful silent auction, vendors, and a rug show of your creations right in the main area of the cells." No solitary confinement here. They may be behind bars but this gang of rug hookers has the joint jumping!

Canton, Mississippi's Old Madison Jail once housed prisoners but is now the annual meeting place of Jail House Rock; hook-in extraordinaire that attracts rug hookers from near and far. Mississippi. 2008. *Courtesy of Lisanne Miller.*

The prisoners left the building in 1969, but the rug hooking, Elvis-loving Jail House Rockers have not. Mississippi. 2008. *Courtesy of Lisanne Miller.*

In the tradition of "The King," whose bust and album grace the breakfast buffet, the morning meal at Jail House Rock leaves little to be desired. Mississippi. 2008. *Courtesy of Lisanne Miller.*

Once inside the main jail, set up for the hook-in begins. Rug hookers gather to hook, chat, and enjoy the day's events. Mississippi. 2008. *Courtesy of Lisanne Miller.*

A vintage radio in the jailers' quarters was used to display hooked and photographic portraits of a special young lady. Mississippi. 2008. *Courtesy of Lisanne Miller.*

Displayed in the jailers' quarters are hooked rugs of all shapes and sizes. Mississippi. 2008. *Courtesy of Lisanne Miller*

MISSISSIPPI

Hooking artists embrace the Christmas holidays with a variety of hooked Santas. Mississippi. 2008. *Courtesy of Lisanne Miller.*

Put up your feet and stay a while...not a phrase that any prisoner would want to hear. Fried eggs crown a hen hassock hooked by Faith Williston. Mississippi. 2008. *Courtesy of Lisanne Miller.*

Hooked rugs on display and ready for viewing. Mississippi. 2008. *Courtesy of Lisanne Miller.*

Becki Cumbie's hooked "Home Coming" brings a note of hope to this jail house setting. Mississippi. 2008. *Courtesy of Lisanne Miller*.

Elvis beckons you to take a break from hooking and sample a cinnamon roll or two. Mississippi. 2008. *Courtesy of Lisanne Miller.*

On display, as you exit the jailer's quarters, is a hooked reminder that you are now leaving the "Land of the Free;" a grim thought for those who once called the "Big House" home. Hooked by Jane Becker. Mississippi. 2008. *Courtesy of Lisanne Miller.*

The harsh and grim conditions of the Old Madison Jail are in sharp contrast to the cheerful enthusiasm of dedicated rug hookers. Mississippi. 2008. *Courtesy of Lisanne Miller.*

Christasia, granddaughter of hooking artist Sandra Holmes, came to Jail House Rock and worked on a design of her own. Rug hooking has become a family tradition. Mississippi. 2008. *Courtesy of Lisanne Miller.*

Behind bars. Hooking artists at work. Mississippi. 2008. *Courtesy of Lisanne Miller.*

Vendors offered a wide variety of hooking supplies including patterns and colorful woolen fabrics. Mississippi. 2008. *Courtesy of Lisanne Miller.*

Overcrowding is no problem for Jail House Rock. The more the merrier. Mississippi. 2008. *Courtesy of Lisanne Miller.*

It's time for lunch; Elvis, Southern hospitality, and good food. Who could ask for more? Mississippi. 2008. *Courtesy of Lisanne Miller.*

Finding that perfect pattern brightens this rug hooker's day. Mississippi. 2008. *Courtesy of Lisanne Miller.*

A view from the guard's cat walk shows rug hookers immersed in their work. Mississippi. 2008. *Courtesy of Lisanne Miller.*

Absorbed in her work, Sandra Holmes hooks a colorful abstract paisley design. Mississippi. 2008. *Courtesy of Lisanne Miller.*

In addition to rug hooking, friends, fine food, and loads of fun there are also door prizes, goody bags and a silent auction for those doing time at Jail House Rock. Pictured in blue is Lisanne Miller, director of the event and president of The Magnolia Wool Dust Society; the Mississippi chapter of ATHA (Association of Tradition Hooking Artists). She hands a surprise gift to a lucky recipient. Mississippi. 2008. *Courtesy of Lisanne Miller.*

Prison bars become a makeshift display rack for this handsome geometric design hooked rug. Mississippi. 2008. *Courtesy of Lisanne Miller.*

By mid-afternoon Jail House Rock was jumping with rug hookers. Mississippi. 2008. *Courtesy of Lisanne Miller.*

Where did that come from? A Jessie Turbayne book at Jail House rock. Southern hospitality at work! Mississippi. 2008. *Courtesy of Lisanne Miller.*

Pictured is rug hooking artist Jacque Juvenal and her well-endowed "Mermaid," the talk of this jail house gathering. By raising and sculpting the hooked loops that form this sea siren's chest, Jacque has given her creation an enhanced bust line. Mississippi. 2008. *Courtesy of Lisanne Miller.*

Lockdown doesn't seem to bother these confined rug hooking artists as the day draws to a close. No jailbreaks were reported and a good time was had by all. Mississippi. 2008. *Courtesy of Lisanne Miller.*

Laverne Hellums

An old time "Saint Nicholas," with tree in hand, heralds the coming of Christmas. Pine trees and stars form decorative corner motifs. Polly Minick design. Hooked by Laverne Hellums. 2008. Mississippi. 29" x 30". *Courtesy of Laverne Hellums.*

For her first hooking project, "Cape Cod Primitive" Laverne Hellums chose, with the help of her teacher Faith Williston, a subtle yet cheerful color scheme. Harry M. Fraser Co. pattern. Hooked by Laverne Hellums. Mississippi. 2007. 31" x 65". *Courtesy of Laverne Hellums*.

A bi-colored "Garden Hare" bolts through a turning and twisting vine. Designed by Charles Gay. Hooked by Laverne Hellums. Mississippi. 2008. 27.5" x 32". *Courtesy of Laverne Hellums.*

Deborah Feldman

Nothing says Mississippi like a slice of cool watermelon on a hot afternoon. And this "Watermelon Chair Pad" not only reminds us of a summertime favorite it offers a soft place to rest our weary bones. Designed by Jacque Juvenal. Hooked by Deborah Feldman. Mississippi. 2007. Diameter 13". *Courtesy of Deborah Feldman.*

Imaginary birds, a touch of Jacobean design, and note of whimsy form a "Fantasy Floral Tote Bag." Designed by Susan Quicksall / Holly Hill Designs. Hooked by Deborah Feldman. Mississippi. 2007. 9" x 13". *Courtesy of Deborah Feldman.*

"I hooked 'Eeny, Meeny, Miney Hooked Hats' as a shower gift for my daughter whose wedding date is near Halloween." A witch's broomstick made of twigs is used as a decorative hanger. Lacey Jane Primitives. Hooked by Deborah Feldman. Mississippi. 2008. 10" x 27". *Courtesy of Deborah Feldman.*

Maureen Boswell

With homes in Mississippi and Texas, Maureen Boswell chose to hook a tribute to the Lone Star State. In front of the Alamo, and behind flowering blue bonnets, "Texas Pups" pose for their woolen portrait. Pictured are the family pets; a Soft Coated Wheaten Terrier and, complete with bandana, an Australian Cattle Dog, the beloved dog of yesteryear's Texas cattlemen. Western symbols including a cowboy hat, boots, and star are hidden in the hooked loops. Designed by Sibyl Osicka. Hooked by Maureen Boswell. Mississippi and Texas. 2008. 25" x 33". *Courtesy of Maureen Boswell.*

Today's rug hooking artists are often inspired by Oriental rug designs. Using traditional colors, the blue field of this "Early Caucasian Carpet Bag" was hooked in a horizontal manner to mimic the weaving of a woven rug. New Earth Designs. Hooked by Maureen Boswell. Mississippi and Texas. 2005. 15" x 28". *Courtesy of Maureen Boswell.*

"My granddaughter, 'Anna Caroline' was avoiding having her photograph taken for a Christmas card when she decided to 'play' with her toy mixer in my kitchen. I slipped in and snapped a picture. She was four at the time." Adapted from a photograph. Designed by Bev Conway. Hooked by Maureen Boswell. Mississippi and Texas. 2006. 40" x 24". *Courtesy of Maureen Boswell.*

Sue Burns

Adapted from an antique rug, "'Geometric Star' was my first rug. I had wanted to learn to hook since the early 1980s when I met an elderly lady from Alabama who was a rug hooker. She gave me her accumulated wool and three of her rugs. I learned about Donna Holdiness's Oxford Rug Camp and now I am hooked!" New Earth Designs pattern. Hooked by Sue Burns. Mississippi. 2007. 24" x 36". *Courtesy of Sue B. Burns.*

"Jolly Halloween," the joint effort of two hooking artists, was given to a mutual friend who loves the haunting holiday. A whimsical black cat, flanked by carved pumpkins, issues in the spooky 2008 season. Designed by Kris Miller. Hooked by Sue Burns and Deborah Feldman. Mississippi. 2008. 16.5" x 26". *Courtesy of Sue B. Burns.*

Native Mississippian Sue Burns was inspired and encouraged to become a rug hooker in the 1980s by Mary Frances Baxley of Alabama. Now deceased, the senior rug maker placed three of her prized hooked possessions in Sue's hands, including this original grid design with flowers. Using hand-dyed woolen fabrics throughout the rug, the mottled outer border echoes many of the colors used within. Designed and hooked by Mary Frances Baxley. Alabama. 1949. 37" x 52". *Courtesy of Sue B. Burns.*

Favoring an outer border similar to the aforementioned rug, the late Mrs. Baxley of Alabama hooked a simple spray of posy-like flowers and placed them on a variegated neutral field. The simple yet charming rug is now at home in Mississippi. Designed and hooked by Mary Frances Baxley. Alabama. 1950s. 40" x 24". *Courtesy of Sue B. Burns.*

"Compass Star," given to Sue Burns in the 1980s, led her to rug hooking, a tradition she continues to enjoy today. A series of braided borders frame and protect the hooked star center. Designed and hooked by Mary Frances Baxley. Alabama. 1950s. Diameter 51". *Courtesy of Sue B. Burns.*

Cheerful and colorful, "Circles and Squares" was fashioned from "'as is' found wool and leftover strips from hooking friends. My husband's coat was used for the border." Searsport Rugs. Hooked by Sue Burns. Mississippi. 2008. 32" x 41". *Courtesy of Sue B. Burns.*

Sandra Holmes

Red sky at night.... sailor's delight. Inspired by her collection of nautical beacons, "Sunset on the Light House" was Sandra Holmes's first attempt at rug hooking. "I love it." Designed and hooked by Sandra Holmes. Mississippi. 2008. 19" x 30". *Courtesy of Sandra J. Holmes*.

Ruby Lee Ammons

Using a design often associated with French heraldry, "Fleur-de-Lis Weeps" was hooked to symbolize the pain, sorrow, and destruction that Hurricane Katrina brought to the Gulf Coast region. Designed by Lisanne Miller. Hooked by Ruby Lee Ammons. Mississippi. 2007. 12" x 14.5". *Courtesy of Ruby Lee Ammons.*

"Boo Boo, My Dog," a hooked portrait of a favorite furry friend. Designed and hooked by Ruby Lee Ammons. Mississippi. 2008. 17" x 13". *Courtesy of Ruby Lee Ammons.*

'Sis' Meeks

"What would I hook for my very first rug? You think of the time it will take to hook, the pattern, the wool, binding, the 'over all' cost and then, thinking years ahead, who may cherish this rug. After a few days of thought I had it all planned out. It would be a very simple prayer rug of a 'Descending Dove' – representing the Holy Spirit. Since it is a prayer rug, I wanted my Pastor and friends to bless it and pray over it. I have taken it to several prayer vigils to be used. It stays on the floor upstairs where it is quiet and easy to go to." Inspired by the image of a dove on a church bulletin and drawn into a pattern by Faith Williston. Hooked by 'Sis' Meeks. Mississippi. 2004. 29" x 30.5". *Courtesy of 'Sis' Meeks.*

"Hands of Love." "I wanted to hook a 'family rug' so I decided to hook each person's hands. In my hand, I have hooked a heart for the family 'cause they are my heart. I connected them all with the cross." Designed by Faith Williston. Hooked by 'Sis' Meeks. Mississippi. 2005. 26" x 31". *Courtesy of 'Sis' Meeks.*

"How much we love our grandchildren! This is Madaleine, my first grandchild and first granddaughter and how proud I am of her. I wanted to do a portrait of Madaleine and I was told to get in touch with Victoria Ingalls. What a lovely and talented teacher she is. I went to two workshops with Victoria. In the first one (2004) I just worked on her face. I missed the next year because of Hurricane Katrina. The following workshop I hooked the hair. Madaleine was so much fun to hook. The picture was taken at the beach when she was seven years old. I love this age. If you look closely you can see her missing tooth." The hooked portrait was given to Madaleine on November 9, 2008; her fifteenth birthday. Adapted from a photograph and made into a pattern by Victoria Hart Ingalls. Hooked by 'Sis' Meeks. Mississippi. 2007. 15" x 12". *Courtesy of 'Sis' Meeks*.

Special gifts for granddaughters Madaleine Page Meeks and AnnaGrace Finney Meeks. "Both girls were able to watch as Nana hooked their pillows. Hopefully one day they will be in a 'special place' as a remembrance of how loved my girls are." Designed by Faith Williston. Hooked by 'Sis' Meeks. Mississippi. 2005. 14" x 14". *Courtesy of 'Sis' Meeks*

An adopted daughter of the South, Candace Ballard tells her rug hooking tale.

I became a rug hooker long before I ever pulled a loop. Way back in 1981, I was walking down Madison Avenue in New York City with my sister-in-law when we came upon a show window featuring antique baby furniture with a hooked rug in bright grass green on the floor bringing the fantasy "baby's room" together. I came to a screeching halt like those roadrunner cartoons. Not that the furniture was exquisite, of course it was, but the rug was what gave the display heart and charm, its warmth. I was seven months pregnant with John and I wanted that rug so badly. The price was $600 – might as well have been $6,000, because I wasn't going to get it. Years later I found the same pattern in the DiFranza catalog: "Noah's Ark." I made it with teacher Diane Stoffel's help and it went into the "baby's" room when he was sixteen.

We were living in Plainfield, New Jersey when John was born and as a toddler he made friends with an adorable little boy named Henry Whipple Farnum, IV…Whip! One heavenly fall afternoon, Whip's mother and I took the boys down a little back lane to her mother's house. I had no idea what was ahead of me; we were just out having a walk with our children on a glorious day. But the house when we came to it was a perfect gem – center chimney cape with grayish cedar shakes on the sides, white trim, and powder blue shutters. Inside there must have been more than twenty hooked rugs all over the floors, set off with perfect taste. Yes, the furniture was fabulous…secretary, Windsor chairs, simple crewel and muslin curtains, all of it…I have never seen a more beautiful home. Ever…including my own. But then suddenly, I had taste too. Instantly acquired. Because that was it! It was the rugs that gave those rooms their real beauty. I stared and stared. Didn't even have to try to be sophisticated and nonchalant about it…I was bowled over and said so. "Oh, Nancy," I remember saying, "you made these rugs! How? I've never seen anything so lovely. Would you show me how to make them?"

"No," she said firmly. "You and Priscilla have more than enough to do raising your boys. You don't have time to hook rugs." She then said that you didn't just hook the rugs; you had to dye the wool yourself. Somehow I got the impression of stooping over hot vats of dye, making colossal messes that "ServPro" would charge double time to clean up. Anyway, she succeeded in discouraging me. But every time I visited that house, it was the rugs that I visited, and their colors that I remembered.

In 1987, Tom got a job in Jackson, Mississippi, that brought us here to live and made us into Mississippians. Getting here – proved kind of fun. I was to drive down to Jackson with the dogs, taking three leisurely days to do it, and Tom and John were to fly to Jackson on the weekend. Saying goodbye to Plainfield was hard for me, because I loved it there. Until then I had been a Midwesterner. On my way out of town I stopped at a little bookstore downtown, which had been one of my favorite haunts, to say goodbye. On one of the display tables featuring local authors was a smallish book, called *The Hook Book* by Alice Beatty and Mary Sargent. I almost cried when I found out that they lived less than five miles away, that they taught rug hooking, and even had groups coming to their homes to hook together. At night, after a long day of driving down to Jackson, I pored over that book with the dogs flaked out on the bed with me.

I didn't order the equipment right away – obviously moving into our house came first. But in the back of the book were the names and addresses of places where you could buy wool and dyes, hooks and frames. And then one day, I went for it! The business I chose was Braid Aid, in Massachusetts. Mrs. Griswold took my call … she became a friend at that moment. I bought everything I used from them until they closed a few years ago. No one could have been kinder in leading me through the intricacies of setting up to be a rug hooker. She sent me a Puritan frame, a Bliss cutter, a Susan

Bates hook, the patterns "Shaker Tree" and "Cape May Primitive," several yards of wool and two dyes: Cushing's Reseda Green and Egyptian Red. I loved it! Playing in a sandbox as a child is a joy similar to it. Overall, rug hooking answers my needs at every pitch. When I feel like creative playing I dye wool; when I feel like doing something or getting on with things, I hook; And when I am tired and wiped out, I go to bed and look at pictures of all the rugs I'd like to make if there were but world enough and time.

After maybe ten years of rug hooking on my own, I learned about a rug camp at Tezcuco Plantation, outside Baton Rouge. I went and loved it. And since then I have been to several camps – six, I think, altogether. Carrie Martin, a friend I met at Tezcuco camp, suggested I go to Teachers' Workshop because there aren't many teachers in Mississippi. I learned about shading the first year, which was such a breakthrough. Charlotte Price, Pat Chancey, Nancy Blood, and Dot Schutte were my teachers there and the improvement in my work was demonstrable after that first year.

There really isn't much more to tell. I'm no teacher, but still love rug hooking. Right now I am working on a rug to hang in the Mississippi Craftsmen's Gallery on Rice Road in Madison, Mississippi. Because I am not a Southerner, not a Mississippian by birth, I wanted to choose my words of homage to our adopted state with care. After a few false tries, I found a book called *Lanterns On the Levee* by William Alexander Percy, which has the sort of language I was looking for in my tribute. I've already hooked the words: "The Mississippi… more beautiful and dear to its children than Thames or Tiber…it abides, aloof and unappeasable, with no heart except for its own task, under the unbroken and immense arch of lighted sky, where the sun, too, goes a lonely journey." The background is to be a sunset on the river, with golden light shimmering over the water. I've seen it a hundred times…if only I can capture it for the rug.

Rug hooking artist Candace Ballard was commissioned by her friend Bettye Mason to hook a rug as a surprise for her husband Dick's 65th birthday. "The placement of the items on the border wasn't in any particular order, but intended to be like snapshots around the house and family and their pets. Bettye had a watercolor of the children, which I copied for their clothes and relative sizes for the front porch. Then I began hooking the little vignettes. For instance, Dick took the Concorde to Paris so we 'borrowed' a model of it from his office to get the right tip for the nose. They took a family vacation to Alaska, hence the Totem Pole (he brought it back with him), New York City, and lots of trips to the beach. His favorite football team is Dallas. He's played golf at St. Andrew's and won the golf tournament, thus the trophy. And he loves to fish. He was in the oil business, graduated from Oklahoma, sent his children to Jackson Prep, here in town (colors red and white). Dick was in Korea during the war. The church window represents the church where he and Bettye now worship. His favorite car was a blue BMW." The hooked story lives on. "The Mason Rug." Designed and hooked by Candace Ballard. Mississippi. 2001. 36" x 42". *Courtesy of Candace Ballard.*

"I made this rug for our son's first apartment after he graduated from college. The olive tones are hooked from a Marine blanket belonging to my husband's father during his service in World War II. I used it sparingly – keeping some back so I could incorporate it into more rugs." "Desert Wanderer." Designed by Jane McGown Flynn. House of Price / Charco pattern. Hooked by Candace Ballard. Mississippi. 2004. 43.5" x 86.5". *Courtesy of Candace Ballard.*

An image of the Old South, "Hauling the Whole Week's Pickings." "I really like Pris Buttler and made this pattern after studying with her at camp." Pris Buttler Designs. Hooked by Candace Ballard. Mississippi. 2003. 20" x 35". *Courtesy of Candace Ballard.*

"I made this rug for a woman who has been our close friend for more than twenty years. She collects cranberry glass, so I tried to match the color for her." "Wilton Rose Heroic." Lib Callaway patterns. Hooked by Candace Ballard. Mississippi. 1995. 28" x 62". *Courtesy of Candace Ballard.*

"Lillie Aline." "I made this rug for a friend's first grandchild who was named for her two great grandmothers! What a Southern sounding name!" Country ABC Rugs designed by Mary Ellen Wolff. Sunnybrook Design. Hooked by Candace Ballard. Mississippi. 2007. 18" x 72". *Courtesy of Candace Ballard.*

"Our Bible Study group meets every Wednesday afternoon at Kathy Hays's house, having come together in her living room for more than a dozen years. We all wanted to do something to show her how much this privilege means to us; something unique and personal. Isn't it amazing how rug hooking so often answers this desire? I offered to do the rug, and the group generously supplied money for materials. It lies before the fireplace in the room where we meet, a labor of love representing all of us (with our initials hooked into the branches).

"Kathy spent her childhood in Gulfport, Mississippi; graduated from Vanderbilt University (The Commodore is reaching down from his augustness to pat her on the head!) I had to waylay her husband one day to find out the date of their wedding, and he added to my store of knowledge of her life by telling me that they had lived in Germany for several years, and that they had a sailboat, named the 'Kathy B' which took them all around the Gulf in their salad days. Their cat Tigger, taking a bow, has a sparkler in his paw. In order to hook him I needed the help of Kathy's neighbor, who captured Tigger in an unwary moment and held him up so I could examine his tummy for accuracy in portrayal. The rose window represents our church. And, of course, the circle of faces is our group." "Kathy Hays Rug." Designed and hooked by Candace Ballard. Mississippi. 2005. 28" x 72". *Courtesy of Candace Ballard.*

"The Bennett Rug." "This rug was a commissioned rug for a fiftieth wedding anniversary. The Bennetts have four children, three of them married, six grandchildren, with all of them needing to be pictured in the rug. In addition, Dr. and Mrs. Bennett had grown up and been childhood sweethearts in St. Augustine, Texas. He had played football and she had been a drum majorette. During the Korean War, he joined the Navy and served on the 'Intrepid.' When I began hooking that section, my husband asked what number it was. I'm sure I looked blank, and Tom said everything in the military has a number. Mrs. Bennett had no idea when I asked her, but Tom assured us that Dr. Bennett would know. So at that moment the rug stopped being a surprise, because when Mrs. Bennett asked him, he came out with it instantly, after more than fifty years. Dr. Bennett was also in medical school at the University of Texas. (As a practical difficulty I couldn't keep all the schools and the ship on Dr. Bennett's 'side' of the rug because all those buildings would have thrown off the balance of the rug. So the timeline of events is out of order.) Another thing, too, Dr. Bennett's residency at Parkland Hospital in Dallas ended just a few months before President Kennedy was brought there, dying, in November 1963. He knew everyone who attended him that day.

"A couple of things in the second half of the rug. Dr. Bennett and Mrs. Bennett took special training to become communion servers in the church, because their minister is in a wheel chair. Because this is such a central part of their lives, it is the largest section of the rug. Another detail on the left hand side: for her senior project their oldest granddaughter wrote a biography of Mrs. Bennett, which touched her deeply, so I pictured them together with Mrs. Bennett 'reading' the manuscript. A second item is Dr. Bennett with the green Mustang, which he keeps under a tarp in the garage and works on at his leisure along with his two grandsons and their green wagon." Designed and hooked by Candace Ballard. Mississippi. 2005. 26" x 72". *Courtesy of Candace Ballard.*

"I've made a thousand or more ornaments through the years. Last year, when I was selling my ornaments at the Craftsmen's Guild of Mississippi, one of my customers made a comment that I should hook all different kinds of dogs, instead of just labs and poodles. One of my neighbors, who have a Springer spaniel, ordered ten. Santas and angels are still my best sellers, and I am always looking for unusual shapes and outfits for both." Designed and hooked by Candace Ballard. Mississippi. 2008. Ornaments range in size from 2" to 3" high. *Courtesy of Candace Ballard.*

"The Johnson Rug." "My friend, Elizabeth Johnson, is a very well known artist here in Jackson. We agreed to make a trade – a hooked rug for a portrait of our son, John. Dick Johnson is a surgeon, so I portrayed him with his partner Walter Jones, performing an operation. They love the beach and the artist's studio has John's portrait on the easel as their cat laps up the paint spattered about. The church, in the upper left corner, is the First Presbyterian Church here in Jackson, where Dick and Elizabeth have sung in the choir for more than twenty years. The verses around the border are from Shakespeare, 'King John' and say: 'He is the half part of a blessed man, left to be finished by such as she; and she, a fair divided excellence, whose fullness of perfection lies in him.' That's just how I feel about them." Designed and hooked by Candace Ballard. Mississippi. 1995. 36" x 72". *Courtesy of Candace Ballard.*

OXFORD RUG CAMP
Oxford, Mississippi

Each year, in early November, rug hookers gather in Oxford, Mississippi, to attend rug camp. Located just 80 miles from Memphis, in autumn this college town boasts warm breezy days and a colorful landscape of rolling hills. The University of Mississippi, the "Ole Miss" Blues Archive, which houses the personal collection of blues legend B. B. King, and author John Grisham all call Oxford home. Rowan Oak, pre-Civil War estate of the late William Faulkner is another local attraction. With so much to see and do, combined with Southern hospitality, good food and the camaraderie of fellow hooking artists, it is easy to see why Oxford Rug Camp is such a popular destination.

Held at the Downtown Oxford Inn, camp revolves around five days of instruction and a variety of classes from a changing roster of teachers. Classes start at nine in the morning with a one-hour break for lunch. Then back to work until "Daddy Comes Home" which is around four. According to camp director, Donna Holdiness, "Now... it does depend on how hard everyone has worked that day – sometimes he gets home a little early." And the "happy hour" begins. Classrooms stay open at night and seeing enthusiastic students working on their rugs after midnight is not an unusual sight.

Rug hookers embrace life. They love to laugh, learn from other rug makers, and share the joys of their craft. Oxford Rug Camp offers the perfect stage for all three.

Photographs of Oxford Rug Camp are courtesy of Scott Burton Photography / Oxford, Mississippi.

The Oxford Rug Camp – class of 2008. Mississippi. *Courtesy of Donna M. Holdiness.*

Whether in the classroom or during free time, students at the Oxford Rug Camp are dedicated to their rug hooking. Mississippi. 2008. *Courtesy of Donna M. Holdiness.*

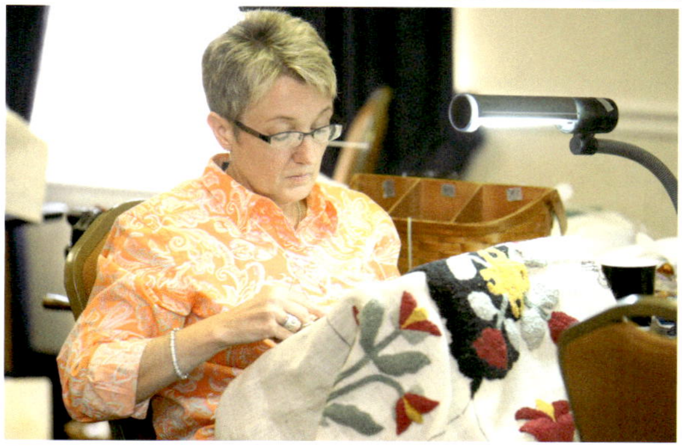

MISSISSIPPI

Oxford Rug Camp founder and director, Donna Holdiness stands between rug hooking teachers Jeanne Benjamin of Massachusetts and Sibyl Osicka of Ohio. Taking a break from their daily hooking, rug makers enjoyed a field trip to Rowan Oak, novelist William Faulkner's historic Mississippi home. 2008. *Courtesy of Donna Holdiness*.

Donna Holdiness

"I started hooking because my best friend wanted us to do this together. We have had many fun days." Donna Holdiness's first project was this colorful "Christmas Star Stocking." Pattern maker unknown. Hooked by Donna Holdiness. Mississippi. 1999. 15" x 6". *Courtesy of Donna M. Holdiness.*

"Fruit," a delightful touch of color for any dining room or kitchen floor, wall or tabletop. A dozen solo cherries add a note of whimsy. Primco pattern. Hooked by Donna Holdiness. Mississippi. 2003. 30" x 22". *Courtesy of Donna M. Holdiness.*

Charging "Moose," hooked for Donna's youngest son, are portrayed on backgrounds of colorful blocks. Superimposing one background over the other creates an optical illusion of depth. Designed by Heart and Hands. Hooked by Donna Holdiness. Mississippi. 2003. 29" x 44". *Courtesy of Donna M. Holdiness.*

FAITH WILLISTON – OCEAN SPRINGS, MISSISSIPPI

After traveling the country with her husband and three sons, landscape painter and hooking artist Faith Williston came to Ocean Springs, Mississippi. A certified McGown teacher, Faith teaches locally and conducts ongoing classes at her home. "Everyone seems to know about landscape painting, yet few know about traditional rug hooking." Thanks to Faith more and more are learning to "paint with wool."

"Flowers and Stars" is a primitive design executed in a festive manner. Bits of bright color and the glow of two stars add a lively touch. Reminiscent of hooking techniques used in the late 19th century, artist Faith Williston fashioned her rug with strips of woolen fabric cut into 8/32" wide strips. Pris Buttler Designs. Hooked by Faith Williston. Mississippi. 2008. 28" x 38". *Courtesy of Faith G. Williston.*

"Andrew and Melissa Marion came home after Hurricane Katrina to a slab. They lost everything. This broke my heart that my friend had lost her memories. The Marion family bought a home new to them but old and historic to the coastal town of Ocean Springs, Mississippi. When Melissa gave me a tour of the new house it was evident to me that she needed a hooked rug. I hooked this rug so they can build new memories." The design for "Melissa's Home" was adapted from a stained glass window and includes a pineapple, the sign of hospitality and a crab, an important part of the Gulf Coast fishing industry. Hooked by Faith Williston. Mississippi. 2007. 72" x 36". *Courtesy of Faith G. Williston.*

Faith Williston hooked "Summer Garden" for an auction to benefit the Walter Anderson Museum in Ocean Springs, Mississippi. The lucky bidder was Pat Phaff, who was able to enjoy the rug for a while… until Hurricane Katrina hit. Hearing that Faith had lost her own rugs in the devastating storm, Pat gave "Summer Garden" back to the artist who had hooked it. In Faith's words, "That story is just one example of the generosity of people after the storm." Primco pattern. Hooked by Faith Williston. Mississippi. 2004. 28" x 38". *Courtesy of Faith G. Williston.*

A hooked study of the favorite flower of the South, a "Magnolia." Designed by Jane McGown Flynn. House of Price / Charco pattern. Hooked by Faith Williston. Mississippi. 2006. 16" x 16". *Courtesy of Faith G. Williston.*

"My dear friend Lynn, who died from breast cancer, inspired 'East Meets West.' I wanted to remember the happy days spent with her and her family at Mount Vernon and the National Mall in Washington, D.C. She was a great help in planning this rug and she was able to see it finished before she passed." Adapted from a Charco pattern. Hooked by Faith Williston. Mississippi. 1999. 72" x 43". *Courtesy of Faith G. Williston.*

Using strips of woolen fabric cut 6/32" and 8/32" wide, Faith Williston hooked "Antique Bed Rug," replicating yarn sewn designs of an earlier time. Harry M. Fraser Co. pattern. Hooked by Faith Williston. Mississippi. 2008. 38" x 48". *Courtesy of Faith G. Williston.*

Setting a medieval tone, "Cathedral Enchantment" combines flowing linear patterns and angular motifs. Adapted from an old Oriental rug pattern. Designed and hooked by Faith Williston. Hooked by Faith Williston. Mississippi. 2008. 4' x 8'. *Courtesy of Faith G. Williston.*

"Country Hens." "I needed something fun to do and this was it!" Designed by Bev Conway. Hooked by Faith Williston. Mississippi. 2008. 24" x 48". *Courtesy of Faith G. Williston.*

Trish Williams

"Farm House Rooster" is displayed over a fireplace hanging from an antique make-do tool used for grasping out of reach jars. "I love doing scrap rugs from my basket of leftovers, but knew this needed something special in the center. I'd been talking to my friend and teacher, Lisanne Miller, and one day she said, 'How about a rooster?' She knows that I have a collection of roosters… so it was perfect." Designed by Lisanne Miller and Trish Williams. Hooked by Trish Williams. Mississippi. 2008. 30" x 37". *Courtesy of Trish Williams.*

Add a mat and frame and "Scrappy Round-To-It" becomes "pop art." "I'm a frustrated artist. Both of our children are artists and I can't draw a stick man. However, since taking up rug hooking I feel artistic and it truly is a wonderful feeling." Designed and hooked by Trish Williams. Mississippi. 2006. 43" x43". *Courtesy of Trish Williams.*

Libby Sutherland

"Patriotic Bicycle" recalls parades, fireworks and summers in Maine. Multiple stars frame the celebration. Polly Minick pattern. Hooked by Libby Sutherland. Mississippi. 2008. 30" x 48". *Courtesy of Libby Sutherland.*

Using scraps of woolen fabric, Libby Sutherland re-created a popular old "Geometric Hit or Miss" pattern. Adapted from an old design and made into a pattern by Lisanne Miller. Hooked by Libby Sutherland. Mississippi. 2008. 40" x 50". *Courtesy of Libby Sutherland.*

Dressed in polka dots and ready to strut; "Country Hens." A hit or miss border echoes the colors used within. Designed by Bev Conway. Hooked by Libby Sutherland. Mississippi. 2008. 27" x 53". *Courtesy of Libby Sutherland.*

Joanne Humphries

A simple spray of "Strawberries" makes a charming hooked chair pad. Pearl McGown pattern. Hooked by Joanne Humphries. Mississippi. 1957. Diameter 15". *Courtesy of Joanne M. Humphries.*

"'Barnyard King' was started as a rug in the late 1950s. I moved to Mississippi in 1973 where I worked on it off and on. When my rooster was finally finished I sewed him on a pillow made from a World War II army blanket." Designed and hooked by Joanne Humphries. Mississippi. 2008. 18" x 18". *Courtesy of Joanne M. Humphries.*

Jane Dunaway

Stripes, in autumn shades, form a delightful hooked "Pumpkin," complete with woody stem and felted leaf. Designed by Lisanne Miller. Hooked by Jane Dunaway. Mississippi. 2007. 8" high. *Courtesy of Jane Dunaway.*

Linda Bottom

The sun shines down on a "Patriotic Saltbox" painted in shades of red, white, and blue. A question mark curl of smoke rises from the chimney. Designed by Lisanne Miller. Hooked by Linda Bottom. Mississippi. 2008. 14" x 18". *Courtesy of Linda Bottom.*

"'Watermelon Chair' pad is my first hooking project. I am a Mississippian transplanted from Michigan; I lived there my entire life until now. A daughter and three grandsons lured us to the South, where I became a 'Hooker on the Square in Canton, Mississippi.'" Linda is a frequent visitor to Canton's rug hooking haven, "P is for Primitive." Designed and hooked by Linda Bottom. Mississippi. 2008. Diameter 14". *Courtesy of Linda Bottom*.

"It's Light the Way," an impressionistic view of a lighthouse – a beacon of hope and symbol of safety, on and off the water. Designed by Lisanne Miller. Hooked by Patricia Ann Cheeks. Mississippi. 2008. 38" x 26". *Courtesy of Patricia Ann Cheeks.*

Sunny days and "Dragonfly Summer." Designed by Lisanne Miller. Hooked by Patricia Ann Cheeks. Mississippi. 2008. 20" x 12". *Courtesy of Patricia Ann Cheeks.*

Chapter 4

Waltzing Through TENNESSEE

Where would rock and roll and country music be without Tennessee? Aside from its proud history and rich agricultural heritage, Tennessee lays claim to Elvis Presley, Aretha Franklin, Tina Turner, Chet Atkins, Johnny Cash, Dolly Parton, and so many more. Graceland, where "The King" held his Memphis court, is the second most visited home in the United States and Nashville's Grand Ole Opry launched the careers of country music's greatest stars.

"The Volunteer State," so named during the War of 1812 when thousands of Tennesseans enlisted and fought with marked valor, offers monuments, museums, and the Great Smoky and Appalachian Mountains. And like those from the past who stepped forward... the dedicated artists of Tennessee present to you their hooking talents.

Deb Wire

A sweet and simple folk art design; "Two Flowers" and three stars share a lively and vibrant field. Designed by Jen Patek. Hooked by Deb Wire. Tennessee. 2008. 22" x 18". *Courtesy of Deb Wire.*

Flecked with starlight, "Night Time in a Faerie's Garden" invites one and all into an enchanted village dwarfed by fanciful flowers. Designed by Karen Kahle / Primitive Spirit pattern. Hooked by Deb Wire. Tennessee. 2005. 23" x 36". *Courtesy of Deb Wire*.

The colors of fall make for a handsome "1847 Turkey." Needlelove Design. Hooked by Deb Wire. Tennessee. 2007. 19" x 26". *Courtesy of Deb Wire.*

The king of beasts is a symbol of strength. "My dad had a heart attack just after I finished the lion's body. His illness inspired me to keep hooking and finish this rug so that he could see it completed." "Antique Lion." Designed by Karen Kahle / Primitive Spirit pattern. Hooked by Deb Wire. Tennessee. 2008. 25" x 50". *Courtesy of Deb Wire.*

Cynthia Hogg

Fallen from a hooked marbled sky; the "Evening Snow" covers a well-lit, warm, and secluded cabin. Limited color choice makes for a simple, yet charming, runner suitable for floor, wall, or tabletop use. Designed by Diane Gay. Hooked by Cynthia Hogg. Tennessee. 2005. 10.5" x 30". *Courtesy of Cynthia Hogg.*

Bold and colorful diamonds by the half dozen line up for review. "Beginner's First Piece." Designed and hooked by Cynthia Hogg. Tennessee. 2005. 21" x 15". *Courtesy of Cynthia Hogg.*

Light streams through a decorative "Stained Glass Window." Pattern maker unknown. Hooked by Cynthia Hogg. Tennessee. 2007. 24.5" x 16". *Courtesy of Cynthia Hogg.*

Deidra Bailey

Light, bright, dark, and dull; all the shades needed to please the eye. "2007 Scrap Rug." "The only rug I hooked that year! My one year-old son kept me busy." Designed and hooked by Deidra Bailey. Tennessee. 2007. 19" x 31". *Courtesy of Deidra Bailey.*

Complete with a "tweed" melon, this bountiful "Fruit Basket" is framed with a lively lamb's tongue border. Pearl McGown pattern. Hooked by Deidra Bailey. Tennessee. 2004. 22" x 37". *Courtesy of Deidra Bailey.*

"Tabby," was hooked then glued onto wood, making for a quiet, low maintenance feline friend. Designed and hooked by Deidra Bailey. Tennessee. 2004. 13" tall. *Courtesy of Deidra Bailey.*

This hefty, green-eyed cat, with his red ball of yarn, poses on a variegated carpet of wavy design. A sunny and swirling van Gogh-like backdrop highlights the reclining feline as a color filled chain frames the vignette of playful patterns. "Cat Playing With Ball." Primco pattern. Hooked by Deidra Bailey. Tennessee. 2004. 21.5" x 31.5". *Courtesy of Deidra Bailey*.

BY HOOK OR BY CROOK

Crossville, Tennessee

Once upon a time in the year 2000, four lovely ladies, all-living in Crossville, Tennessee, came together to hook rugs. Doris Colegrove, Shirley Johnson, Elaine Morrow, and Barbara Obert met informally, exchanged ideas and began teaching each other how to make rugs. Doris had heard through a friend that a trained rug hooking instructor lived nearby. Doris made a call and Shelley Hoffman, a certified McGown teacher, offered her expertise to the quartet of hooking novices. Overtime word spread about these rug hooking ladies and within a few years time the By Hook or By Crook group grew to over 30 members. Meetings are held the third Wednesday of each month. Members hook, exchange ideas and discuss upcoming exhibits and demonstrations. Desiring more time together, some of the ladies break off into smaller groups and meet weekly. From time to time rug hooking "celebrities" are invited to teach special classes. What rug hooker could ask for more? With a hook in their hands and a smile on their faces all is well in Crossville, Tennessee. And the rug hookers are indeed... living happily ever after.

Ann Crowley

"Cock a Doodle Do" was adapted from an article in a grocery store magazine citing "101 Ways to Cook a Chicken." "I learned to hook in the 1970s – twenty-five years later I took up the art again." Hooked by Ann Crowley. Tennessee. 1995. 22.5" x 33.5". *Courtesy of Ann Crowley.*

Detail of "Cock a Doodle Do." *Courtesy of Ann Crowley.*

This rug was hooked from remnants of other rugs. "So many of my rugs have been given away that each circle of 'Scrappy #2 – This N More That' reminds me of a particular project." Fast food cups were used to draw the circles. Rug hookers are an ingenious lot and like to re-cycle. Designed and hooked by Ann Crowley. Tennessee. 1996. 22.5" x 47". *Courtesy of Ann Crowley.*

Sweet and simple, "Three Little Chicks" came to be because "I had leftover wool." Designed and hooked by Ann Crowley. Tennessee. 1999. 8" x 14". *Courtesy of Ann Crowley.*

Influenced by his dad's work at Delta airlines, a then five-year-old Mathew drew his version of a DC-8 in flight. Mathew's "Plane" was copied, drawn onto monk's cloth and then hooked by his proud rug-making mother. Adapted and hooked by Ann Crowley. Tennessee. 1999. 18" x 20". *Courtesy of Ann Crowley.*

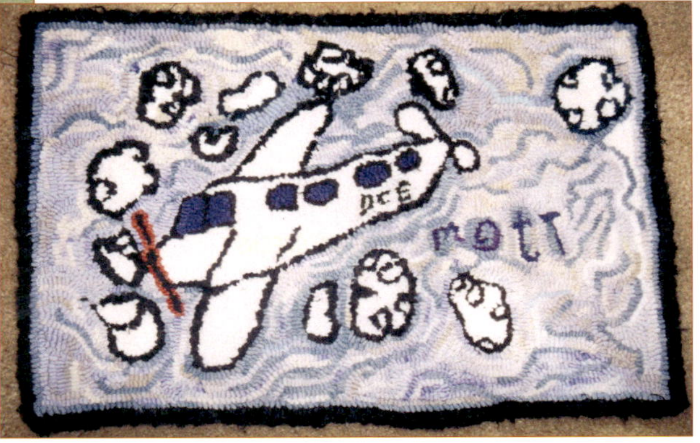

"This whimsical pattern, purchased in Florida, was so much fun to hook. Our daughter-in-law was enchanted with it and it now hangs year-round in their Georgia home." "Joy to the World" features a trio of whimsical gals celebrating winter holidays. Designed by Carol Feeney. Hooked by Ann Crowley. Tennessee. 2002. 32" x 45.5". *Courtesy of Ann Crowley.*

Rest your weary head on "Lady Diana," a pillow design of foxglove and scrolling. Designed by Jane McGown Flynn. House of Price / Charco pattern. Hooked by Ann Crowley. Tennessee. 2008. 15" x 15". *Courtesy of Ann Crowley.*

Twenty-five hooked animals spell out "Alphapets;" the animal beginning with the letter "X" remains a question. A teaching tool to delight both young and old. Designed by Muzzy Petrow. Hooked by Ann Crowley. Tennessee. 2007. 54" x 32". *Courtesy of Ann Crowley.*

"Morris" is a hooked tribute to the nineteenth century socialist, poet, and master of design and style. Adapted from a William Morris design. Pattern maker unknown. Hooked by Ann Crowley. Tennessee. 2000. 32" x 44". *Courtesy of Ann Crowley*.

Detail of "Morris." *Courtesy of Ann Crowley.*

Barbara Obert

Another interpretation of the aforementioned "Lady Diana." Designed by Jane McGown Flynn. House of Price / Charco pattern. Hooked by Barbara Obert. Tennessee. 2008. 14" x 14". *Courtesy of Barbara Obert.*

"Butt Grandma" is the product of a creative and stylish grandmother whose grandchild needed a decorative boost in their chair. Designed and hooked by Barbara Obert. Tennessee. 2002. 13.5" x 15". *Courtesy of Barbara Obert.*

Becky Schnepf

In 2003, after watching one of Nova Scotia's Cheticamp mat makers hook, Becky Schnepf was convinced that she had to hook rugs too. Locating an instructor just 13 miles from her Tennessee home, she learned the craft on a simple design before attempting to hook a likeness of "Deputy Doo Dah," her mule. "I had never designed anything but knew exactly how I wanted Doo's rug. With a blown up head shot and tracings of his bit and shoe, my instructor drew them on linen and dyed my wool. I designed the background. I am so pleased. I've been hooking ever since and love it." Designed and hooked by Becky Schnepf. Tennessee. 2005. 17" x 29". *Courtesy of Becky Schnepf.*

Detail of "Deputy Doo Dah." *Courtesy of Becky Schnepf*.

Bonnie Willis

"Lady Diana," a favorite rug hooking pattern, covers the top of an antique stool. Designed by Jane McGown Flynn. House of Price / Charco pattern. Hooked by Bonnie Willis. Tennessee. 2008. Diameter 16". *Courtesy of Bonnie Willis.*

"I was asked by our group, By Hook or By Crook, to present a program on 'Alternative Materials for Rug Hooking.' Having experimented successfully using denim fabric and yarns, I looked forward to the challenge. I did research, visited thrift stores and raided closets!" Nylon stockings, lace, yarns, corduroy, ribbons, tulle, tee shirts, velvets, trash and grocery bags, man-made fleece and sheep fleece were used. "Each petal of the design is hooked in unique materials." Designed and hooked by Bonnie Willis. Tennessee. 2006. 21" x 30". *Courtesy of Bonnie Willis.*

The backside of "Alternative Materials for Rug Hooking." *Courtesy of Bonnie Willis.*

Charisse Straight

A learning tool, "The Practice Bunny" pattern is a first project given to novices joining the By Hook or By Crook rug hookers. Designed by By Hook or By Crook members. Hooked by Charisse Straight. Tennessee. 2008. 12" x 12". *Courtesy of Charisse Straight.*

Adapted from an "Old Christmas Card," an attentive kitty, complete with thread whiskers, follows a rotund tree and star holding Santa. This jolly old fellow sports a soft, fuzzy white beard. Hooked by Charisse Straight. Tennessee. 2008. 12" x 12". *Courtesy of Charisse Straight.*

Darlene Elkins

"Cats Relaxing" was "inspired by 'our' cats and the places they find to sleep. I started rug hooking late in 2007 and have been enjoying it ever since. I learned a lot about color matching during my quilting days." Designed and hooked by Darlene Elkins. Tennessee. 2008. Each 16" x 18". *Courtesy of Darlene Elkins.*

Debbie Beeman

Under the guidance of Georgia hooking artist and instructor Eric Sandberg, "Canterbury Cottage" came to life. Elegantly framed, the hooked landscape depicts the cottage on Canterbury Lake where Debbie Beeman lives. This piece, a first year project for Debbie, utilizes a variety of advanced hooking techniques. Adapted from a photograph by Eric Sandberg. Hooked by Debbie Beeman. Tennessee. 2008. 10" x 14". *Courtesy of Debbie Beeman.*

Doris Colegrove

"'Stars' was my first rug. I drew it on a piece of burlap and cut the wool with scissors." A simple and pleasing design and welcomed note of color for wall, tabletop or floor. Designed and hooked by Doris Colegrove. Tennessee. 2000. 28" x 32". *Courtesy of Doris Colegrove.*

"Good Morning" rooster is perched on a wooden fence and surrounded by a lively checkerboard frame. This proud barnyard king, complete with multicolored plumage, was hooked from re-cycled woolen fabric. Designed by Chloe. Hooked by Doris Colegrove. Tennessee. 2000. 28" x 26". *Courtesy of Doris Colegrove.*

Detail of "Appliquéd and Hooked." *Courtesy of Doris Colegrove.*

Woolen fabric "tongues," embroidered and adorned with antique buttons, frame a hooked center. The small central motif of stylized flowers joins an op art array of colorful circles of concentric design. "Appliquéd and Hooked." Adapted from a Primitive Pastimes pattern. Hooked by Doris Colegrove. Tennessee. 2004. 16" x 21". *Courtesy of Doris Colegrove.*

"'Safari' is my favorite rug." Under the tutelage of Maine hooking artist and teacher, Jacqueline Hansen, Doris Colegrove learned the Waldoboro technique of raising and sculpturing your hooked loops. "Each animal has some Waldoboro hooking; the elephant's trunk, hippo's tail, frog's eyes, etc. I loved this class." Designed by Kathy Moulds. Hooked by Doris Colegrove. 36" x 48". *Courtesy of Doris Colegrove.*

Detail of "Safari" shows the raised portion of the lion's mane. *Courtesy of Doris Colegrove.*

This "Running Horse" adds color and comfort to a wooden bench. Note the swirling movement created when Doris hooked the background field. Designed and hooked by Doris Colegrove. Tennessee. 2007. 15" x 22". *Courtesy of Doris Colegrove.*

Two bunnies hide. Floating blossoms and buds mingle with an array of foliage and help to camouflage the furry duo. An inward facing scalloped edge secures "The Secret Garden." Designed by Karen Kahle / Primitive Spirit pattern. Hooked by Doris Colegrove. Tennessee. 2002. 32" x 34". *Courtesy of Doris Colegrove.*

Detail of "The Secret Garden." *Courtesy of Doris Colegrove.*

"Woman on the Path." "I did this rug in memory of my mother, who, like rug designer Deanne Fitzpatrick, was born in Newfoundland and raised in Nova Scotia. I am sure my mother would be pleased with it." Designed by Deanne Fitzpatrick. Hooked by Doris Colegrove. Tennessee. 2008. 34" x 22". *Courtesy of Doris Colegrove.*

Hit or miss stripes of bright color echo the colors used to hook "Pomegranate." Adapted from picture found in a book. Hooked by Doris Colegrove. Tennessee. 2001. 23" x 36". *Courtesy of Doris Colegrove.*

There's nothing more American than buying a hooked rug pattern at a garage sale on a Saturday morning. And that's just what Doris Colegrove did. "American Flag." Pattern maker unknown. Hooked by Doris Colegrove. Tennessee. 2003. 26" x 34". *Courtesy of Doris Colegrove.*

Detail of "American Flag." *Courtesy of Doris Colegrove.*

Elaine Morrow

Crowing too early and you've reached "The Wrong Number." Not everyone wants to rise at the crack of dawn but this finely feathered rooster seems to enjoy his job. Patsy Becker pattern. Hooked by Elaine Morrow. Tennessee. 2002. 25" x 38". *Courtesy of Elaine Morrow.*

"Mammoth Flower" pillow was hooked using strips of woolen fabric cut 1/2" wide. To achieve floral details rug hookers often hook with # 3 (3/32") and #4 (4/32") cuts of wool. Harry M. Fraser Co. pattern. Hooked by Elaine Morrow. Tennessee. 2003. 15" x 15". *Courtesy of Elaine Morrow.*

Detail of "Mammoth Flower." *Courtesy of Elaine Morrow.*

"Sing a Song of Six Pence" illustrates a beloved children's nursery rhyme. A limited use of color, distributed throughout the rug, makes for an aesthetically pleasing hooked design. Morton House Primitives. Hooked by Elaine Morrow. Tennessee. 26" x 35". *Courtesy of Elaine Morrow.*

Jacqueline Westerbeck

A circling school of gold fish frame contented cats, "Taffy and Geeker." Adapted from a photograph. Designed and hooked by Jacqueline Westerbeck. Tennessee. 2008. 15.5" *Courtesy of Jacqueline Westerbeck.*

"Winkie" depicts a very special one-eyed cat. "I saw him get thrown out of a car and I picked him up and took him home." Working from a photograph, Jacqueline Westerbeck's first hooked piece, a chair pad, portrays the striped feline survivor encircled by a parade of mice. One out of step mouse heads in the opposite direction. Designed and hooked by Jacqueline Westerbeck. Tennessee. 2008. Diameter 15.5" *Courtesy of Jacqueline Westerbeck.*

LuAnn Patterson

First introduced to rug hooking by a college roommate in 1975, LuAnn Patterson became truly "hooked" in 2004 when she was invited to join a beginner's group. In addition to hooking, "I have been interested in antiques, period clothing, and customs for as long as I can remember. The first colonial pocket pattern I came across was a crewel design. When I saw this 'Colonial Pocket with Bunny' it was a natural for me to complete. I use it to hold by rug hooks and scissors." *Rug Hooking* magazine pattern. Hooked by LuAnn Patterson. Tennessee. 2004. 12" x 7". *Courtesy of LuAnn Patterson.*

About to hook her next piece, "I proudly told my friends and fellow hookers that I planned to start slowly and not jump in. I planned to use only recycled wool and free or hand-drawn patterns. Within ten minutes of my statement I had purchased this pattern on monk's cloth and some hand-dyed wools." "Froggin' Around," complete with tassel, was LuAnn Patterson's second project. Designed by Bev Conway. Hooked by LuAnn Patterson. Tennessee. 2004. 10" x 10". *Courtesy of LuAnn Patterson.*

Detail of "Froggin' Around." *Courtesy of LuAnn Patterson.*

Lynne Baker

"This was my first rug project, done to go in my guest bedroom. Unfortunately, by the time I completed the rug, I had sold the house and no longer had the guest bedroom. 'Grandmother's Garden' went on the kitchen floor for a few years and now hangs over the toilet in the laundry room. A comment, perhaps, on my early skills." Pattern maker unknown. Hooked by Lynne Baker. Tennessee. 2001. 26" x 42". *Courtesy of Lynne E. Baker*.

"Apples." "This was my second rug project. By the time I completed it I saw the wisdom of using a color palette more expanded than blue and yellow." Pattern maker unknown. Hooked by Lynne Baker. Tennessee. 2002. 28" x 44". *Courtesy of Lynne E. Baker*.

"Zephyr." A masterful use of color accounts for an exemplary Oriental-style hooked rug. Charco patterns. Hooked by Lynne Baker. Tennessee. 2005. 39" x 57". *Courtesy of Lynne E. Baker.*

Detail of "Zephyr." *Courtesy of Lynne E. Baker.*

"I took 'Grapes' to rug hooking camp three years in a row before I finally had the ability and appropriate teacher to start on it. It was so tedious to work on the grapes that I dragged the project out for almost three years before completing it. I have not hooked another grape since and I rarely eat them!" Designed by Bev Conway. Hooked by Lynne Baker. Tennessee. 2005. 36" x 40". *Courtesy of Lynne E. Baker.*

Detail of "Grapes." *Courtesy of Lynne E. Baker.*

A raised and sculptured hooked bunny tries to enter a crazy quilt-like field. Floral and foliage panels are separated by a combination of hooking and needlework. Lynne Baker used Jacqueline Hansen's "Crazy Quilt" pattern for the background and added a little cottontail rabbit. "The Secret Garden." Hooked by Lynne Baker. Tennessee. 2006. 24" x 41". *Courtesy of Lynne E. Baker.*

Detail of "The Secret Garden." *Courtesy of Lynne E. Baker.*

Detail of "No Sister I." *Courtesy of Lynne E. Baker.*

"These rugs are for my granddaughters. The 'Oh well, no sister' phrase was coined by the youngest granddaughter several years ago when we were on a family vacation on Amelia Island in Florida. I was walking with the two girls (age 5 and 7) on the dock after dinner. Emily's hand was firmly clasped in mine but Hannah, the elder and more predictable of the two, walked on her own. Suddenly I lost sight of Hannah and in a panic voice asked, 'Emily, Where's Hannah?' Emily showing typical concern for her older sister, glanced around briefly, shrugged her shoulders and announced with an evil grin, 'Oh well, no sister!' Since that time 'Oh well, no sister' is announced at all appropriate moments – whenever one of them appears to be in danger of falling, drowning, or otherwise meeting an untimely end... or when one gets to do something wonderful and the other, for whatever reason, does not. Despite their moments of spite, the two are also close friends and buddies. The rugs attempt to depict both spectrums of sisterhood through the 'shadow people' as well as the primary figure." "No Sister I and No Sister II." Designed and hooked by Lynne Baker. Tennessee. 2008. Each 46" x 32". *Courtesy of Lynne E. Baker.*

"I did 'The Cottage' in three days and gave it to my Mom for Valentine's Day. Using many of the cottage prints hanging on my walls for inspiration, I drew my own cottage. I worked feverishly and added a bit of 'hooving up' here and there." "Hooving up" is an old term often used to describe the technique of pulling your hooked loops higher than usual, forming a raised area. Designed and hooked by Lynne Baker. Tennessee. 2007. 14"x 11". *Courtesy of Lynne E. Baker*.

Detail of "The Cottage." *Courtesy of Lynne E. Baker.*

"This runner-sized rug was originally a purchased pattern for a Chinese rug to which I had applied and partially hooked the rope border. I started hooking the pattern numerous times and simply did not like it. I finally pulled everything out, cut leaf shapes out of brown paper bags and drew the new design in about twenty minutes. I then dyed a series of dip-dyes in 'fall' colors, as I see them – pinks, aquas, greens, yellows and golds. It is my favorite rug." "Falling Leaves." Designed and hooked by Lynne Baker. Tennessee. 2008. 71" x 30". *Courtesy of Lynne E. Baker.*

Margaret Minick

"Basting Beauties" recalls youthful days and summertime fun. Stripes, polka dots, and footprints in the sand make for a lively scene. Going Grey pattern. Hooked by Margaret Minick. Tennessee. 2008. 26" x 34". *Courtesy of Margaret Minick.*

Margie Parko

"I bought a New England saltbox replica on a lake in Tennessee. An artist, who originally owned the house, had painted a mural of a whaling scene over the upstairs fireplace. I designed my 'Whale Rug' to complement the mural. This is my first hooked piece. As a retired educator, I like the creativity involved in designing my own projects. I also like the idea of re-cycling old woolen clothes and hooking with them." Designed and hooked by Margie Parko. Tennessee. 2008. 24" x 36". *Courtesy of Margie Parko*.

Mary Lou Knowles

Using a pattern found at a garage sale and hooking with all re-cycled wool, Mary Lou Knowles crafted her own "Field of Flowers." This was her first hooked rug. Pattern maker unknown. Hooked by Mary Lou Knowles. Tennessee. 1998. 21.5" x 38". *Courtesy of Mary Lou Knowles.*

"Sally in the Flowers" sports a thick and raised coat. Laying your hooked loops in an every which way pattern, often referred to as the anti-godlin-style of hooking, accounts for her "wooly" look. Pattern maker unknown. Hooked by Mary Lou Knowles. Tennessee. 2005. 23" x 28". *Courtesy of Mary Lou Knowles.*

Detail of "Sally in the Flowers." *Courtesy of Mary Lou Knowles.*

"Six Stars," decorated and placed in spotlights of color, makes for a simple yet charming geometric rug. The wavy ribbon border mirrors the colors used to hook the stars and circles. Designed by Kris Miller / Spruce Ridge Studios. Hooked by Mary Lou Knowles. Tennessee. 2005. 21.5" x 27.5". *Courtesy of Mary Lou Knowles.*

Honoring 60 years of marriage, Mary Lou Knowles hooked her "Peaceful" tribute using woolen yarn to hook the sheep's heads. Pris Buttler Designs. Hooked by Mary Lou Knowles. Tennessee. 2007. 19.5" x 32.5". *Courtesy of Mary Lou Knowles.*

Paula Rehorst

"Hooking is only one of my artistic medias. My Dad was a watercolor/oil artist. I followed with his artistic abilities only with cloth, thread, wool, and yarn." "Wild Rose." Harry M. Fraser Co. pattern. Hooked by Paula Rehorst. Tennessee. 2002. Diameter 14.5". *Courtesy of Paula Rehorst.*

Reflecting on the design's origins and meaning, Paula Rehorst selected a simple palette to hook her "Shaker Tree of Life." Mountain Handcraft Company. Hooked by Paula Rehorst. Tennessee. 2004. 24" x 36". *Courtesy of Paula Rehorst.*

Hooking lends itself to many uses other than floor covering and wall hangings. "Pansy Purse." Designed and hooked by Paula Rehorst. Tennessee. 2005. 7.5" x 8". *Courtesy of Paula Rehorst.*

"Blue Bird" was hooked with strips of woolen fabric, fleece, and yarn. Designed and hooked by Paula Rehorst. Tennessee. 2006. 9.5" x 7.5". *Courtesy of Paula Rehorst.*

Shari Smith

Far right:
Cats come out at night and literally swing from the moon. "Crabtree Cats" was Shari Smith's first hooking project. Patsy Becker pattern. Hooked by Shari Smith. Tennessee. 2002. 43" x 25". *Courtesy of Shari B. Smith.*

Detail of "Crabtree Cats." *Courtesy of Shari B. Smith.*

Cat lover and kitten foster mom, Shari Smith understands that "no woman is ever well dressed without cat hair". "Cat Hair." New Earth Designs pattern. Hooked by Shari Smith. Tennessee. 2003. 41" x 27". *Courtesy of Shari B. Smith.*

"'Sam' came to us as a stray and only lived for six years. He was much beloved – much missed." Designed and hooked by Shari Smith. Tennessee. 2003. 32" x 20". *Courtesy of Shari B. Smith.*

"Oslo," a rosemaling design, hooked under the direction of a teacher in training, was Shari Smith's first time hooking with a #3 (3/32") cut strip of woolen fabric. Rosmaling, the traditional Scandinavian style of painting found on walls, furniture, and wooden dinnerware, inspired both rug hookers and pattern makers. Charco pattern. Hooked by Shari Smith. Tennessee. 2003. 14" x20". *Courtesy of Shari B. Smith.*

Rug hookers are into re-cycling and Shari Smith used the lining of her 1954 nursing school cape to hook the background of "Rewards of May." Patsy Becker pattern. Hooked by Shari Smith. Tennessee. 2004. 27" x 34". *Courtesy of Shari B. Smith*.

A vivid purple background highlights an animated black cat and his pumpkin companions. "Jolly Halloween" was made into a pillow and awaits weary trick or treaters. Designed by Kris Miller. Hooked by Shari Smith. Tennessee. 2007. 14" x 22". *Courtesy of Shari B. Smith*.

A bug-eyed hooked fashion first, "Frog Purse" blends a bit of whimsy with functionality. Designed by Anne Eastwood. Hooked by Shari Smith. Tennessee. 2005. 10" x 7.5". *Courtesy of Shari B. Smith.*

"Mammoth Flowers," is a work in progress. When completed, the guest bedroom 3' x 8' rug will showcase favorite shades of purple and green. Harry M. Fraser Co. pattern. Hooked by Shari Smith. Tennessee. 2008. *Courtesy of Shari B. Smith.*

"Give Thanks" reminds us of wind swept harvest time and the first Thanksgiving. Designed by Jane Olson. Hooked by Shari Smith. Tennessee. 2004. 14" x 32". *Courtesy of Shari B. Smith*.

Shirley Johnson

Shirley Johnson was one of the original four "girls" who hooked together and formed Crossville's By Hook or By Crook rug hooking club. Each of the four hooked "Good Morning" and this is her version of the popular pattern. Designed by Chloe. Hooked by Shirley Johnson. Tennessee. 2002. 28" x 26.5". *Courtesy of Shirley Johnson.*

A lamb's tongue edge, embellished with needlework and buttons, frames a lively hooked center. "Appliquéd and Hooked." Primitive Pastimes pattern. Hooked by Shirley Johnson. Tennessee. 2008. 27" x 32". *Courtesy of Shirley Johnson.*

Named for a beloved Tennessee rug hooking teacher, "Ramona's Cottage" was hooked as a gift for Shirley Johnson's daughter. "This is my favorite piece. I learned several new techniques and came up with a much different look." Prairie Craft House pattern. Hooked by Shirley Johnson. Tennessee. 2007. 14" x 10". *Courtesy of Shirley Johnson.*

Suzanne Butler

"My husband is a golf enthusiast. We retired to a golfing community and he has golfed several times a week and participated in leagues and tournaments. When I saw 'The Golfer' pattern I just had to hook it for my husband's office." This dapper fellow, dressed in vintage apparel, has made it to the 19th hole. Designed by Bev Conway. Hooked by Suzanne Butler. Tennessee. 2007. 42" x 30". *Courtesy of Suzanne Butler.*

Charlotte Plummer

"'Give Thanks' was my very first rug. With help and advice from my hooking friends I completed this is just a few weeks... just in time for Thanksgiving." Designed by Jane Olson. Hooked by Charlotte Plummer. Tennessee. 2006. 16.5" x 37". *Courtesy of Charlotte Plummer.*

"Fruit Stand," complete with patriotic flag and lone radish, is a whimsical interpretation of a traditional still life. Naïve and fresh (no pun intended), the design of this odd grouping is an example of hooked Outsider Art. In addition to using strips of woolen fabric, hand-dyed yarn was used to hook the blue background. Designed by Maggie Bonanomi – "Need L Love" Co. Inc. pattern. Designed originally as a quilt pattern. Hooked by Charlotte Plummer. Tennessee. 2007. 18.5" x 23.5" *Courtesy of Charlotte Plummer.*

Under the guidance of Georgia rug hooking teacher, Eric Sandberg, Charlotte Plummer hooked Oregon's "Yaquina Head Lighthouse," using a variety of unique techniques including hooking upside down. Inspiration came from a photograph found in *American Lighthouses* by Jill Caravan. Adapted and designed by Eric Sandberg. Hooked by Charlotte Plummer. Tennessee. 2008. 23" x 20". *Courtesy of Charlotte Plummer.*

Detail of "Yaquina Head Lighthouse." *Courtesy of Charlotte Plummer.*

Lucille Gamelin

"Original Beginner's Pattern" was designed by the members of By Hook or By Crook to practice hooking skills. "I started by going to class and observing. I enjoyed what the ladies were doing and so I joined and finished this project which was my first." Hooked by Lucille Gamelin. Tennessee. 2008. 10" x 13". *Courtesy of Lucille Gamelin.*

Miriam Fenton

Miriam Fenton created "Lady Diana" during a workshop conducted by hooking artist, Shelley Hoffman. The popular pattern was then made into a pillow. Designed by Jane McGown Flynn. House of Price / Charco pattern. Hooked by Miriam Fenton. Tennessee. 2008. 16" x 15". *Courtesy of Miriam Fenton.*

A carpet of roses and kitties painted on her granddaughter's bedroom walls, were motivation for Sharon Smith to fashion "Vivian's Rug." Designed and hooked by Sharon Smith. Tennessee. 2006. 26" x 41". *Courtesy of Sharon Smith.*

"Up in the attic my daughter-in-law found a diagram for 'Wildflower Trellis' and 'tons' of cut wool for a future rug. Using the diagram I designed a round rug and used her grandmother's cut wool to hook this rug for my granddaughter, Vivian Irene Smith." Adapted from a Joan Moshimer pattern. Hooked by Sharon Smith. Tennessee. 2007. Diameter 17". *Courtesy of Sharon Smith.*

Sharon Smith loves to make rug hooking gifts for others. "My aunt and uncle live on a dairy farm in Michigan and I thought it would be fun to do a 'Dairy Cow Pillow' for them. They truly enjoyed the surprise." Sunflowers, some with raised center details, are a favorite snack of a doe-eyed bovine. Designed by Barbara Obert. Hooked by Sharon Smith. Tennessee. 2008. 22" x 24". *Courtesy of Sharon Smith*.

Detail of "Dairy Cow Pillow." *Courtesy of Sharon Smith.*

Under the guidance of Georgia rug hooking teacher, Eric Sandberg the memory of "my husband's grandmother's depot house in Scotland" was transformed into a treasured hooked image. "Ardlui," a hamlet in Argyll and Bute, was adapted from a photograph using a variety of unique rug hooking techniques. Adapted and designed by Eric Sandberg. Hooked by Sharon Smith. 2008. 15" x 21". *Courtesy of Sharon Smith.*

Detail of "Ardlui." *Courtesy of Sharon Smith.*

Stephanie Rhoades

A blue ribbon winner at the Cumberland County Fair; these "Old Buttons" are kept in hooked jar. Designed by Wendy Miller. Hooked by Stephanie Rhoades. Tennessee. 2008. 21" x 12". *Courtesy of Stephanie Rhoades.*

Detail of "Old Buttons." *Courtesy of Stephanie Rhoades*.

Suzanne Morris

"Sand Dollars." "My first project in rug hooking was influenced by a Florida lifestyle." Designed and hooked by Suzanne Morris. Tennessee. 2008. 15" x 18". *Courtesy of Suzanne Morris.*

SHELLEY HOFFMAN – SCROLL MASTER

In 2008 Shelley Hoffman, a certified McGown rug hooking instructor and founding member of the By Hook or By Crook group, offered a workshop on how to hook a finely shaded scroll. Scroll motifs, found on early hooked rugs dating back to the mid-1800s, continue to be a design element popular with rug hookers today. What follows is sampling of the group's very successful first attempt at hooking shaded scrolls.

Shelley Hoffman instructs By Hook or By Crook members on how to hook foxgloves and finely shaded scrolls. "Lady Diana," a 12" x12" Jane McGown Flynn design was the pattern of choice. *Courtesy of By Hook or By Crook*.

Hooked by Anne Crowley. Tennessee. 2008. *Courtesy of Anne Crowley.*

Hooked by Bonnie Willis. Tennessee. 2008. *Courtesy of Bonnie Willis.*

Hooked by Barbara Obert. Tennessee. 2008. *Courtesy of Barbara Obert*.

Hooked by Debbie Beeman. Tennessee. 2008. *Courtesy of Debbie Beeman*.

Hooked by Miriam Fenton. Tennessee. 2008. *Courtesy of Miriam Fenton.*

Hard at work and mastering the art of hooking finely shaded scrolls. *Courtesy of By Hook or By Crook.*

Hooked by Shari Smith. Tennessee. 2008. *Courtesy of Shari B. Smith*

Hooked by Sharon Smith. Tennessee. 2008. *Courtesy of Sharon Smith.*

Detail of Sharon Smith's aforementioned "Lady Diana." *Courtesy of Sharon Smith.*

Hooked by workshop instructor, Shelley Hoffman. Tennessee. 2008. *Courtesy of Shelley* A. *Hoffman.*

Detail of Shelley Hoffman's "Lady Diana." 2008. *Courtesy of Shelley A. Hoffman.*

Hooked by workshop instructor, Shelley Hoffman. Tennessee. 1992. *Courtesy of Shelley A. Hoffman.*

Detail of Shelley Hoffman's "Lady Diana." *Courtesy of Shelley A. Hoffman.*

Hooked by Sue Morris. Tennessee. 2008. *Courtesy of Sue Morris.*

Under the direction of hooking artist, Shelley Hoffman rug hookers hone their skills. *Courtesy of By Hook or By Crook.*

GETTING INVOLVED

CACE – Cumberland Artisans for Creative Expression – is an organization that offers Tennessee artists support and opportunities. As active members of CACE, By Hook or By Crook rug hookers are involved in the much anticipated CACE Expo, Youth Expo, and CACE Home Tour.

The annual Youth Expo showcases artwork from area schools. Local artists are invited to display their work and demonstrate their craft to interested children. The next generation of rug hookers is taught to hook by Mary Lou Knowles, By Hook or By Crook member. Tennessee. 2008. *Courtesy of By Hook or By Crook.*

By Hook or By Crook members display their work at the CACE Expo, Crossville, Tennessee. 2008. *Courtesy of By Hook or By Crook.*

Designed as a group project by Barbara Obert, this hooked rug was auctioned off at the CACE Expo as a means of raising funds to support the arts. A different By Hook or By Crook member hooked each section of the crazy quilt pattern. Tennessee. 2008. 24" x 36". *Courtesy of By Hook or By Crook.*

RHONDA MOLLENKOPF – "HOOKING OUTSIDE THE BOX"

A certified McGown teacher, Tennessee's Rhonda Mollenkopf likes to hook "outside the box." "Every rug I do makes me think."

"This was my first attempt at rug hooking. I wanted something that I would not get bored with. 'Sun and Moon' is an adaptation of a Dan Morris graphic art design, done with his permission. Thank goodness my teacher let me start outside the box. Now I am devoted to rug hooking. Now I host two retreats each year – the Tennessee Rug Hooking Retreat." Adapted from a Dan Morris Design. Hooked by Rhonda Mollenkopf. Tennessee. 2003. 24" x 30". *Courtesy of Rhonda Mollenkopf.*

Focusing on a design motif found in a larger rug of the same name, Rhonda Mollenkopf hooked then mounted "Paisley Hex" inside a mahogany cornice board. The finely shaded piece now graces her bedroom wall. Charo pattern. Hooked by Rhonda Mollenkopf. Tennessee. 2006. 12" x 30". *Courtesy of Rhonda Mollenkopf.*

Using strips of woolen fabric cut 3/32" wide, a "Coral Reef" tropical fish comes to life. Designed by Jane McGown Flynn. House of Price / Charco pattern. Hooked by Rhonda Mollenkopf. Tennessee. 2008. 12" x 16". *Courtesy of Rhonda Mollenkopf.*

KIM NIXON
Maryville, Tennessee

"I try to make any design, my own or someone else's, reflect me. I don't seek to hook something to match someone else's idea. I think it is important to always put your own voice forward. It makes the work more interesting and allows you to make a body of work that stands well together."

Hooking artist Kim Nixon grew up in New Orleans but now resides in Tennessee.

An accomplished artist in her own rite, Kim put down her brush and picked up a hook and the rest, as they say, is history. Her business, Under the Rug, which can be accessed on line, offers Kim's rug and footstool designs and shows her portfolio. Featured here are a few of her hooked footstools.

"Church Stool." "I grew up in New Orleans where there was a bar on every corner. In Tennessee, where I live now, it is a church on every corner. Although they may be the same release they have other things in common too. A roadside bar and a roadside church are both made of cinder block and use some sort of visual gimmick to draw you in. This church is along the 411S towards Atlanta. Its white cinder blocks are transformed into old stonework with erratically painted grout lines. Some of the stained glass windows are painted on too, reminding me of bars that you don't trust leaving alive when the windows are painted over. Possibly underlining the spiritual link between the two." Designed and hooked by Kim Nixon. Tennessee. 2008. 12"W x 17"L x 17"H. *Courtesy of Private Collection.*

"Hot August Night." "This sunflower stool is shamelessly named for a Neil Diamond album but it is also about a perfect summer evening with a good friend and a couple of long rows of standing sunflowers. Getting close and looking into the seed heads as big as my face, I saw those amazing patterns that can be found in nature. Witnessing a moment at the end of that long, hot day dancing with a friend, our arms full of huge flowers is about as good as it gets." Kim Nixon uses "very wide (9/32") strips of wool to hook with because I like the overall mosaic texture it creates for the piece. I also think it is neater to use a really wide strip for say... one of the flower petals in the 'Sunflower Stool.' I dye wool that is very mottled and has colored dyes layered over each other so there is a range of variations in each strip." Designed and hooked by Kim Nixon. Tennessee. 2006. 16"W x 16"L x 16"H. *Courtesy of Private Collection.*

"Say it loud, say it proud. This floral uses a bright intense color as a background. Where I come from beautiful old homes are painted bright pastel colors. Maybe it has something to do with reflecting the heat of our climate or those colors just blend in to the landscape when you squint into all that hot sunshine. You just can't be afraid to make a statement. I developed a floral design that is hooked on top of the stool but transitions to proddy on the sides. The proddy ended up being more like slightly longer cut loops. I liked the shaggy look of the design on the sides compared to the loops on the top." "Floral Stool." Designed and hooked by Kim Nixon. Tennessee. 2006. 17"W x 17"L x 14"H. *Courtesy of Private Collection*.

"Dr. Seuss wrote a book titled *All the Places I Will Go.* 'All the Places I Have Lived' stool looks backward to the different parts of the country I have lived. There is a plantation house with columns for The Deep South, a New York brownstone, a trailer and a church for the Bible Belt, and a couple of indistinct ranch houses for the places in between." Designed and hooked by Kim Nixon. Tennessee. 2007. 14"W x 17"L x 17"H. *Courtesy of Private Collection.*

"Houses can take on the characteristics of their owners. Or maybe people live up to their homes. 'Trailer Stool' is cramped, maybe a little mean, or just down on its luck. It has wheels/casters because this kind of life just isn't as secure as other homes can provide." Designed and hooked by Kim Nixon. Tennessee. 2007. 11"W x 24"L x 16"H. *Courtesy of Private Collection.*

"I loved the name 'Melon Patch' for this old quilt pattern. I did think of a watermelon patch where you have to look to find all the fruit hiding in the big vine leaves. I used the pattern to play with dark and light for that peek-a-boo feeling." "Melon Patch." Rug pattern by Jenny Rupp. Hooked by Kim Nixon. Tennessee. 2007. 18"W x 18"L x 12"H. *Courtesy of Private Collection.*

LAURIE ROBINSON LOVES TO HOOK & HOOK & HOOK...

Tennessee's Laurie Robinson loves her home. She loves her family. And she loves to hook.

I have always been interested in hand work. When I was young, my maternal grandmother taught me to crochet; my paternal grandmother taught me to needlepoint and knit; and my mother taught me to sew. I really like to needlepoint and I sewed out of necessity. I made all my own clothes when I was young, and as an adult, became a professional seamstress for 12 years. I made items for homes through that endeavor, including pillows, bedspreads, dust ruffles, curtains, etc. Over the years, there isn't much I haven't made.

I wanted a new hobby and saw that there was a rug hooking class in my area. I had always admired hooked rugs, but didn't know what was involved. I jumped at the chance to learn. From the very beginning, I loved it! I loved the freedom of it. I could draw my own designs, dye my own colors, and make so many things out of the finished product (like wall hangings, rugs, pillows, etc). I loved the texture of the wool, the different looks achieved when using plaids as opposed to solids, and the unlimited colors available through different dye formulas.

I started making rug after rug, and just couldn't get enough. I have been hooking a little over 10 years and have made well over 100 items. I have about half of them in my house, and more than half have gone to others (mainly family members). I love designing the rug and picking colors but I color plan as I go (I do a lot of taking out). I don't know how I want it to look until I see it, and if I don't think it works, I take it out and try something else. I then pick colors that I think will work for that person, and think about that person the whole time I am hooking. It's so fun! I always have a place the rug will go before I begin designing it, and that determines the style of the rug and the creative thought. I even enjoy finishing the rug, as it is also part of the process. Over the years, I have never gotten tired of it and always have a new design in the wings so I have something new to start as soon as I finish one.

I tried to think of what all I've made over the years but it's hard because I've given so many away and I can't remember them anymore. I have made chair pads, pouches, pillows, wall hangings, floor rugs, piano bench covers, table centers, footstools, a cedar chest cover, Kleenex box covers, Christmas stockings, and several Christmas tree ornaments.

What follows is a small sample of Laurie's handwork... hooked of course! And yes... rumor has it... she does take time to sleep.

Photos courtesy of Scott Robinson.

Tennessee's Laurie Robinson works on one of her many hooking projects. Tennessee. 2008. *Courtesy of Laurie Robinson.*

Busy hands are happy hands; a closer look at Laurie Robinson hooking. Tennessee. 2008. *Courtesy of Laurie Robinson.*

A bird's eye view of Laurie Robinson's kitchen, complete with her "Vase of Flowers" chair pads. Tennessee. 2008. *Courtesy of Laurie Robinson.*

"Vase of Flowers" chair pads. "I wanted to hook pads for my chairs in the kitchen. I definitely wanted them colorful but matching. I chose three different color backgrounds and the same theme – a pot/vase of flowers, then made each a little different." Designed and hooked by Laurie Robinson. Tennessee. 2008. Each 19" x 14". *Courtesy of Laurie Robinson.*

"I wanted something with a big design and a lot of color in front of my kitchen sink, but it also had to be practical. The brown background does the trick. I used the same theme I had used on the chair pads – a vase of flowers – and took some of the flowers from the pads for 'Pot of Flowers Rug.'" Designed and hooked by Laurie Robinson. Tennessee. 2008. 40" x 34". *Courtesy of Laurie Robinson.*

Striving for a warm and friendly atmosphere, "I wanted a rug to welcome people that came in to my kitchen. I also wanted to coordinate with a stained glass lamp I had on my counter 'Kitchen Welcome' fits under my cabinets and next to the lamp." Designed and hooked by Laurie Robinson. Tennessee. 2006. 12" x 21". *Courtesy of Laurie Robinson.*

Another bright spot in Laurie's kitchen. "I made 'Pot of Orange Flowers' early in my rug hooking 'career.' I had just learned to dye wool and tried my skills on this rug. I love color, so being able to dye my own colors was really important." Designed and hooked by Laurie Robinson. Tennessee. 2000. 11" x 10.5". *Courtesy of Laurie Robinson.*

"Van Gogh's Yellow House." "I like van Gogh's paintings and share his same Dutch ancestry, so I decided I would like to hook one of his paintings. This one was not well known but I loved the colors. It was one of my first attempts at hooking." Adapted from "Yellow House" by van Gogh. Hooked by Laurie Robinson. Tennessee. 2000. 17" x 27". *Courtesy of Laurie Robinson.*

Laurie Robinson combined her love of stained glass with her love of rug hooking. "Stained Glass Fruit." Designed and hooked by Laurie Robinson. Tennessee. 2005. 24" x 20". *Courtesy of Laurie Robinson.*

This "Stained Glass Bowl" is highlighted by a colorful checkerboard pattern that was added for "extra interest." Designed and hooked by Laurie Robinson. Tennessee. 2005. 18.5" x 17". *Courtesy of Laurie Robinson.*

"Basket of Palm Trees Rug." "We went on vacation to Florida so I had to do something with palm trees! It gets well used by the back door. My mom asked me what they were – can't everyone see that they are palm trees coming out of a pot!" Designed and hooked by Laurie Robinson. Tennessee. 2006. 31" x 40". *Courtesy of Laurie Robinson.*

Rug hookers are an ingenious lot. "I had just redone my dining room in rust red and teal. I thought a hooked picture tying these two colors together would be nice on the wall. I already had this frame so I made this rug to fit into it." "Two Flower Picture." Designed and hooked by Laurie Robinson. Tennessee. 2001. 14" x 16". *Courtesy of Laurie Robinson.*

Using her decorator's eye, she " wanted another picture of reds, teals, and golds in my dining room. As you can see I love flowers." "Bowl of Fun Flowers." Designed and hooked by Laurie Robinson. Tennessee. 2004. 21" x 27". *Courtesy of Laurie Robinson.*

"We were having a large group over for Thanksgiving and I realized I didn't have anything for the center of the table." Two days later "Pumpkin Table Runner" was in place. Designed and hooked by Laurie Robinson. Tennessee. 2005. 14" x 26". *Courtesy of Laurie Robinson.*

Taking a break from interior decorating, Laurie Robinson heads outside and hooked the likeness of her Franklin, Tennessee home. "My oldest son was leaving for college. I told him I would make a rug to take of anything he wanted. He said he wanted a rug of our home to remember us by." "Our House Rug." Designed and hooked by Laurie Robinson. Tennessee. 2004. 25" x 33". *Courtesy of Laurie Robinson.*

Back inside her home, Laurie Robinson could not wait to hook a rug for "our entry – in front of the front door. It had to be practical because that door is well used. I added a vine running through the background for interest. I tried several different wools so it would have some contrast, but not compete with the main design of flowers." "Flowers and Vine Rug." Designed and hooked by Laurie Robinson. Tennessee. 2004. 43" x 61". *Courtesy of Laurie Robinson.*

"I added an old chair that had been given to me to the entry, but the seat of it was not in good shape. I made this pad to add interest and cover it up; the project took one day." "Tulips Chair Pad." Designed and hooked by Laurie Robinson. Tennessee. 2006. 14" x 14". *Courtesy of Laurie Robinson.*

Gracing both home and hearth with her hooked work, Laurie Robinson crafted "Flowers and Fruit" for in front of the fireplace. Designed and hooked by Laurie Robinson. Tennessee. 2002. 25" x 44". *Courtesy of Laurie Robinson.*

You just can't have enough pillows. "I love making pictorials that aren't detailed. They give the impression of grass and trees without having to make each distinct." "Yellow House Pillow." Designed and hooked by Laurie Robinson. Tennessee. 2005. 12" x 16". *Courtesy of Laurie Robinson.*

"Lilies of the Valley" was the beginning of many pillows. "I had just started hooking and wanted to make a pillow. I used to sew professionally so I didn't see this as a problem." Designed and hooked by Laurie Robinson. Tennessee. 2000. 16" x 17". *Courtesy of Laurie Robinson.*

"My ancestors are from The Netherlands and our family went to visit the 'homeland.' I loved all the row houses in Amsterdam where no one has draperies, just lace curtains with windows that you can see right through the whole house to the other side – hence the blue in the windows is the same as the sky." "Amsterdam Picture." Designed and hooked by Laurie Robinson. Tennessee. 2002. 9" x 21". *Courtesy of Laurie Robinson.*

No sofa is complete without comfy and cozy hooked pillows and a complementary hooked wall hanging. All hooked and designed by Laurie Robinson. Tennessee. 2008. *Courtesy of Laurie Robinson.*

Welcome to Franklin, Tennessee; hometown of rug hooking artist Laurie Robinson. 2008. *Courtesy of Laurie Robinson.*

"I wanted to make a rug based on the town I've lived in for more than twenty years. I love the downtown of Franklin with all its old buildings – so that's what I hooked. These are all parts of the actual buildings on Main Street. Franklin is a very old town and was central to the Civil War so there is a lot of history here." "Franklin, Tennessee." Designed and hooked by Laurie Robinson. Tennessee. 2007. 18" x 31". *Courtesy of Laurie Robinson.*

Examples of classic architecture are found in historic Franklin, Tennessee. 2008. Courtesy of Laurie Robinson.

Laurie Robinson and her hooked rug…live from downtown Franklin, Tennessee. 2008. *Courtesy of Laurie Robinson.*

"This was the first rug I ever made. I was inspired from a design I saw on an old pattern." Laurie's "Tree of Life" hangs above a trio of towels. Designed and hooked by Laurie Robinson. Tennessee. 1999. 17" x 24". *Courtesy of Laurie Robinson.*

Hooked for her daughter, "Max" pays tribute to a special dog. Designed and hooked by Laurie Robinson. Tennessee. 2001. 18" x 19". *Courtesy of Laurie Robinson.*

"I wanted to make a wall hanging for my bedroom and, of course, my favorite design is a vase of flowers. This time I made a variation on that theme by totally stylizing the tulips and adding contour echoing in the background." "Crazy Tulips Rug." Designed and hooked by Laurie Robinson. Tennessee. 2005. 18" x 24". *Courtesy of Laurie Robinson.*

"With speed and little money, I redecorated our master bath." 'Cozy Houses' was completed in a few days." Designed and hooked by Laurie Robinson. Tennessee. 2005. 17.5" x 13". *Courtesy of Laurie Robinson.*

"'Fun Flowers' coordinates with the aforementioned 'Cozy Houses.' This rug also took a few days to make. The wide cuts certainly help with speed." Laurie hooked with strips of woolen fabric cut 9/32" wide. Designed and hooked by Laurie Robinson. Tennessee. 2005. 19.5" x 20.5" *Courtesy of Laurie Robinson.*

Using a foundation of plastic mesh and leftover strips of wool from the aforementioned "Cozy Houses" and "Fun Flowers," the tireless decorating diva Laurie created "Warm Flowers Kleenex Cover." Designed and hooked by Laurie Robison. Tennessee. 2005. 10" x 4". *Courtesy of Laurie Robinson.*

"I made a lot of pillows for myself and family. Several of my rug hooking friends wanted to see how to make them. I hooked this and another design and made them into pillows as they watched. 'Crewel Pillow' took two days to make." Designed and hooked by Laurie Robinson. Tennessee. 2003. 13" x 16". *Courtesy of Laurie Robinson.*

"We had a chance to redo our bathroom on short notice because someone became available to do it. I made 'Three Pots Rug' in two days. I got some fun floral towels so I made this rug to co-ordinate with them." Designed and hooked by Laurie Robinson. Tennessee. 2008. 17" x 21". *Courtesy of Laurie Robinson.*

"Three Pots Rug" in place. Designed and hooked Laurie Robinson. Tennessee. 2008. *Courtesy of Laurie Robinson.*

"I made this 'Blue Flowers Kleenex Box Cover' to match the bathroom towels and the 'Three Pots Rug.'" Designed and hooked by Laurie Robinson. Tennessee. 2008. 4" x 10". *Courtesy of Laurie Robinson.*

A welcomed bit of comfort; "Circles Foot Stool." Designed and hooked by Laurie Robinson. Tennessee. 2005. 11.5" x 14". *Courtesy of Laurie Robinson.*

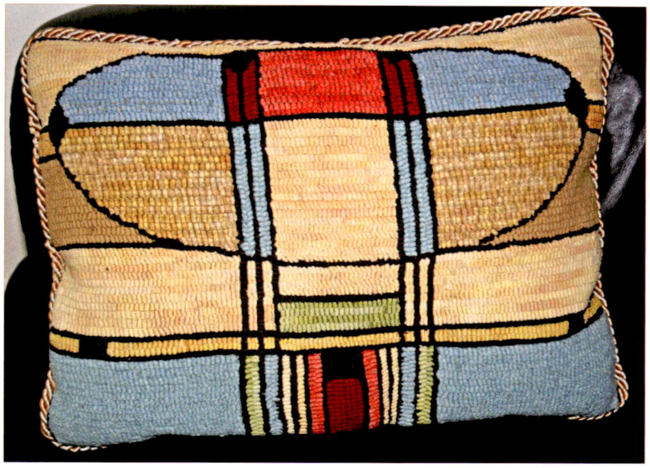

"I needed some pillows for our new leather couch. I thought an 'Arts and Crafts Oval Design' would be something different and interesting." Designed and hooked by Laurie Robinson. Tennessee. 2005. 16" x 22". *Courtesy of Laurie Robinson.*

"Arts and Crafts Diagonals Pillow" was hooked to co-ordinate with the aforementioned "Arts and Crafts Oval Design" pillow. Designed and hooked by Laurie Robinson. Tennessee. 2005. 16" x 22". *Courtesy of Laurie Robinson.*

"My sister was diagnosed with breast cancer. I wanted to do something for her to help her through a difficult time. She loves sunflowers and designed a 'Sunflower Rug' for me to hook." Designed by Ellen Vant Hof. Hooked by Laurie Robinson. Tennessee. 2002. 24" x 36.5". *Courtesy of Laurie Robinson.*

Sharing a love of stained glass, Laurie Robinson presented her sister with two hooked pillows, "Tulip" and "Dancer." Designed and hooked by Laurie Robinson. Tennessee. 2002. 21" x 20" and 12" x 16". *Courtesy of Laurie Robinson.*

Another hooked pillow for sister Ellen. "Bulb." Designed and hooked by Laurie Robinson. Tennessee. 2004. 21" x 21". *Courtesy of Laurie Robinson.*

"Our family spent a weekend with my brother's family at their new log cabin in the woods. My sister-in-law had it decorated so cute that I had to make 'Summer Cabin' for them as a thank you gift." Designed and hooked by Laurie Robinson. Tennessee. 2002. 14" x 13". *Courtesy of Laurie Robinson.*

"A few years later, we went back to visit my brother's cabin but this time it was winter and we were going skiing with them. I hooked 'Winter Cabin' ahead of time as a thank you for the visit." Designed and hooked by Laurie Robinson. Tennessee. 2005. 14" x 16.5" *Courtesy of Laurie Robinson.*

A gift for a brother and sister-in-law; "They wanted a piano seat cover. I chose this design because these are the first two measures of Bach's 'Jesu, Joy of Man's Desiring,' which Dirk sang at my wedding." "Music – Piano Seat Cover." Designed and hooked by Laurie Robinson. Tennessee. 2005. 14.5" x 30". *Courtesy of Laurie Robinson.*

After her parents moved to a new condo Laurie Robinson made "Bird's Nest Tree." "My dad asked me to hook a cover for their cedar chest since it now would be very prominent. I coordinated this design with the rest of the room." Designed and hooked by Laurie Robinson. Tennessee. 2007. 20" x 50". *Courtesy of Laurie Robinson.*

Inspired by wallpaper style and colors, Laurie Robinson hooked "Crewel Flowers Rug" for her parents' house. They now have it in their condo bathroom. Designed and hooked by Laurie Robinson. Tennessee. 2003. 26.5" x 44.5". *Courtesy of Laurie Robinson.*

"My mom inherited this foot stool from her mother. The original needlepoint design had gotten threadbare so she wanted something new. Not wanting to lose her mother's original work we just covered over it. This tulip design harkens back to our Dutch heritage." "Tulip Foot Stool Cover." Designed and hooked by Laurie Robinson. Tennessee. 2001. 20" x 16". *Courtesy of Laurie Robinson.*

"50 Year Anniversary Tree Pillow," on the left, was a gift for Laurie's parents. "Each branch is a different child of theirs – they had six children. On that branch are the flowers for how many people are in that family. Blue is for boys and red is for girls. On the right is "Stylized Flowers Pillow." "I love color and usually the more the merrier. I thought I would try to make a pillow for my mom that had limited colors. It was a fun exercise and different than usual for me." Both designed and hooked by Laurie Robinson. Tennessee. 2001. 13" x 21" and 14" x 18". *Courtesy of Laurie Robinson.*

"'Square Tulip' and 'Triangle Tulip' pillows were made for my parents as a house-warming gift for their new condo. I was recovering from my second back surgery and was house bound." Designed and hooked by Laurie Robinson. Tennessee. 2007. Each pillow is 13" x 21". *Courtesy of Laurie Robinson.*

"We had a family reunion for both my parents' 80th birthdays. My cousin graciously let us use her twenty-five plus bedroom lodge in Northern Michigan. We had such a great time in this gorgeous setting. I made 'Triple Lakes Lodge Rug' as a thank you." Designed and hooked by Laurie Robinson. Tennessee. 2008. 16" x 21". *Courtesy of Laurie Robinson.*

To be admired by all at Triple Lakes Lodge. 2008. *Courtesy of Laurie Robinson.*

"When my niece had her first child, a boy – the first of the next generation in our family – I had to celebrate by hooking a 'Joshua Steven Birth Rug.' I was told the nursery had a night sky décor so that's also my theme." Designed and hooked by Laurie Robinson. Tennessee. 2001. 26" x 30". *Courtesy of Laurie Robinson.*

"When my niece had a little girl, I had to make a rug to celebrate her birth. I was told the nursery was decorated with bugs, so I played on that theme!" "Alyssa Nicole Birth Rug." Designed and hooked by Laurie Robinson. Tennessee. 2004. 22" x 16". *Courtesy of Laurie Robinson.*

"'Pink and Green Lizard Pouch' holds cut wool when I travel with my rug hooking." Shown are both sides of the same pouch. Designed and hooked by Laurie Robinson. Tennessee. 2001. 8" x 11". *Courtesy of Laurie Robinson.*

"I enjoyed making my 'Lizard Pouch' so much I made this 'Black Floral Pouch.' I keep embroidery floss and a punch needle in this one." Shown are both sides of the same pouch. Designed and hooked by Laurie Robinson. Tennessee. 2001. 7" x 10.5". *Courtesy of Laurie Robinson.*

"Checked Vase of Flowers." "This was a really fun rug to make! My sister wanted a red and white checked rug. She also has a lot of blue in her family room. Add to this that she has a home floral business. (She puts flowers in vases all the time!) I tailored this to her." Designed and hooked by Laurie Robinson. Tennessee. 2008. 30" x 36". *Courtesy of Laurie Robinson.*

The aforementioned "Checked Vase of Flowers" resting in front of the fireplace. 2008. *Courtesy of Laurie Robinson.*

Continuing to honor their heritage, "I hooked 'Dutch Tiles Rug' for my sister. Inspiration came from the blue and white delft tiles that decorate her fireplace." Designed and hooked Laurie Robinson. Tennessee. 2001. 26" x 46.5". *Courtesy of Laurie Robinson.*

"Dutch Tiles Rug," mirrors favorite tiles. 2008. *Courtesy of Laurie Robinson*.

And the sunsets in the west as Laurie's parents hold hands and look over their front yard at Lake Michigan. "Looking at the Lake Picture." Designed and hooked by Laurie Robinson. Tennessee. 2008. 9" x 12". *Courtesy of Laurie Robinson.*

RAMONA'S STUDENTS

Chattanooga, Tennessee, was home to Ramona Maddox, a beloved rug hooking artist and teacher who touched the hearts of many, including this author. Ramona delighted in spreading the joys of the craft she loved and was responsible for introducing rug hooking to hundreds of enthusiasts in The Deep South and beyond. She founded and for thirty years directed Castle in the Clouds Rug Hooking School on Lookout Mountain in Georgia, a much anticipated week-long event that welcomed rug hookers from across the United States and Canada. Sadly, in 2008 she quietly passed away after a day of teaching at Little House, her Chattanooga studio. Ramona's students continue to hook rugs under the guidance of Sheri Bennett.

Barbara Holt Hussey

"'Polar Sky' was one of the first pieces in which I experimented with non-traditional hooking materials such as metallic fabric and translucent nylon. I was pleased with the results after using eyelash yarn, metallic fabric and actually encasing some of the wool strips in a sheer fabric." W. Cushing and Company pattern. Hooked by Barbara Holt Hussey. Tennessee. 2005. 16" x 20.5". *Courtesy of Barbara Holt Hussey.*

"'Owl in the Pines' is a project that I finished rather quickly following my move from rural New England to the South. I started hooking with a local ATHA (Association of Traditional Hooking Artists) group within a month of my arrival in suburban Chattanooga. When I saw the owl pattern I knew I wanted to hook a woodsy scene. Once the owl was in good order, I started to consider the background. It was October and much too warm for a New Englander. My fellow hookers warned me not to expect any snow. I made my own by creating a snowy background in this work and it helped to ease my transition into this new environment." Designed by Bev Conway. Hooked by Barbara Holt Hussey. Tennessee. 2007. 28" x 32". *Courtesy of Barbara Holt Hussey.*

"After moving I discovered that many of the flowers from my garden in New England would not grow this far south including the lupines that were a staple in northern gardens. 'Lupines By the Sea' was a piece I had struggled with for a few years before my move. The flowers were very difficult to capture with the 'as-is' wool that I had been using. The influence of other hookers in our local ATHA (Association of Traditional Hooking Artists) chapter caused me to experiment with a variety of dyed wools that turned out to solve the problem." Designed by Deanne Fitzpatrick. Hooked by Barbara Holt Hussey. Tennessee. 2007. 18" x 33". *Courtesy of Barbara Holt Hussey.*

Nancy Diegel

A pleasing folk art design combines "Birds and Pomegranates". Edyth O'Neill Design. Hooked by Nancy Diegel. Tennessee. 2007. 24" x 42". *Courtesy of Nancy Diegel.*

A rustic angel doll, stuffed in a stocking, holds the key to your heart. Circles and half circles made up of concentric bands of color add a note of whimsy to "The Stocking Was Hung." Pattern maker unknown. Hooked by Nancy Diegel. Tennessee. 2007. 32" x 17". *Courtesy of Nancy Diegel.*

Rug hookers are often influenced by what other rug hookers are doing. While at the ATHA (Association of Traditional Hooking Artists) biennial in New Orleans, Nancy saw rug hooking artist and teacher, Vivily Powers hooking "Miniature Oval Oriental" and had to hook one for herself. Designed by Seth Blood. Hooked by Nancy Diegel. Tennessee. 2008. 16" x 28". *Courtesy of Nancy Diegel.*

Bold and bright flowers, of a primitive style, spring forth from a subdued gray vase. "Ipswich." Edyth O'Neill Design. Hooked by Nancy Diegel. Tennessee. 2006. 27" x 34". *Courtesy of Nancy Diegel.*

"Cape Cod," hooked in rich earthy tones, is a favorite pattern in the North and The Deep South. Harry M. Fraser Co. pattern. Hooked by Nancy Diegel. Tennessee. 2007. 32" x 60". *Courtesy of Nancy Diegel.*

Lively hit or miss stripes of color merge and surround "Star Geometric." Designed by Sheri Bennett. Hooked by Nancy Diegel. Tennessee. 2008. 12" x 30". *Courtesy of Nancy Diegel.*

Under the direction of hooking artist and teacher Ramona Maddox, Nancy Diegel hooked her first project, "Santa and Mrs. Claus Kissing" in a romantic winter wonderland setting. Pattern maker unknown. Hooked by Nancy Diegel. Tennessee. 2003. 22" x25". *Courtesy of Nancy Diegel.*

Set on an earth-toned background, a pair of interlocking cornucopias holds a "Bountiful" array of folk art blooms, blossoms, and foliage. Holly Hill Designs. Hooked by Nancy Diegel. Tennessee. 2007. 29" x 46". *Courtesy of Nancy Diegel.*

"Little Bit," with fluffy "poofed" out top and tail, captures the image of a beloved pampered pooch on a pillow portrait. Hooking loops were pulled high, cut, and sculpted to achieve the three-dimensional effect. Designed by Elizabeth Black. Hooked by Nancy Diegel. Tennessee. 2006. 16" x 23". *Courtesy of Nancy Diegel.*

"Giant Flower" evokes images of bright and sunny summer days. Pattern maker unknown. Hooked by Diana Bagby. Tennessee. 2008. 17" x 17". *Courtesy of Diana Bagby.*

Using a monochromatic palette, "Delft" was inspired by the blue and white motifs of Dutch pottery. Pattern maker unknown. Hooked by Diana Bagby. Tennessee. 2008. 31" x 16". *Courtesy of Diana Bagby.*

"Empress" is an elegant example of a Persian-style hooked rug. "This is the one that did me in and took seven years to complete." Pearl McGown pattern. Hooked by Diana Bagby. Tennessee. 1979. 38" x 70". *Courtesy of Diana Bagby.*

Carrying on a Legacy – Sheri Bennett

I started out hooking in 1995 after taking a class at the "International Quilt Festival" in Houston, Texas. After a move to Kentucky, I discovered Ramona Maddox in Chattanooga and started driving down for classes with her. My first two rugs started with her made it into *Celebrations,* a publication of juried hooked art and "Rhapsody in Rugs," a juried exhibit held at the Carnegie Center for Art and History, New Albany, Indiana. After Ramona's death in 2008 I bought her rug hooking supply inventory and opened From Crook to Hook Wool Studio in Chattanooga. We all miss Ramona, but her legacy lives on here in Chattanooga with all of the rug hookers that she taught throughout the thirty some years of her love affair with rug hooking.

What follows is a small sampling of rugs hooked and continuing to be hooked by students of Ramona Maddox.

Southern hospitality and a "Hadley Welcom" await all who visit Sheri Bennett's "From Crook to Hook Wool Studio" in Chattanooga, Tennessee. The decorative motif of this demilune rug, complete with written word, gives nod to early American design. Edyth O'Neill Design. Hooked by Sheri Bennett. Tennessee. 2006. 23" x 37". *Courtesy of Sheri J. Bennett.*

A full service shop, "From Crook to Hook Wool Studio" offers individual instruction, classes, and workshops. Hooking enthusiasts will find a wide variety of patterns and hooking wools, including those hand-dyed treasures that all rug hookers covet. Chattanooga, Tennessee. 2008. *Courtesy of Sheri J. Bennett*.

"Swirly Pot" was aptly named for its curlicue vase motif, twisting vine tendrils, scalloped frame, contoured background and rounded outer corners. Designed by Margo White. Hooked by Sheri Bennett. Tennessee. 2003. 24" x 31". *Courtesy of Sheri J. Bennett*

One circle and three striped fans frame the naïve portrait of a rather rotund "Primitive Sheep" with accompanying stars. The artist's initials appear in the lower right hand corner of the contour hooked background. Woolley Fox pattern. Hooked by Sheri Bennett. Tennessee. 2004. 14.5" x 26". *Courtesy of Sheri J. Bennett*.

"Oh My!" It's a cat, with a crazy hat and rippling smile, emerging from a carved pumpkin. Happy Halloween! Designed by Not Forgotten Farm / Lori Brechlin. Hooked by Sheri Bennett. Tennessee. 2008. 20" x 21". *Courtesy of Sheri J. Bennett.*

"Squares and Bars" was started in a design class with artist, Pris Buttler. A collection of leftover scraps was used to hook this lively geometric pattern. Designed and hooked by Sheri Bennett. Tennessee. 2008. 33" x 53". *Courtesy of Sheri J. Bennett.*

"I had too many scraps so I designed 'Star Geometric' to complement the aforementioned 'Squares and Bars.'" Designed and hooked by Sheri Bennett. Tennessee. 2008. 12.5" x 30". *Courtesy of Sheri J. Bennett*.

"The Mighty Oak," resplendent in the colors of fall, is complemented by a hooked plaid border and series of color coordinating braids. Designed by Sally Kallin. Braiding by Terri Schaefer. Hooked by Sheri Bennett. Tennessee. 2008. 34" x 8' 6". *Courtesy of Sheri J. Bennett.*

Shirley Evans

Ornate scrollwork frames a springtime centerpiece of "Dogwood" and pussy willows. "This was my first piece." Pattern maker unknown. Hooked by Shirley Evans. Tennessee. 2008. 30" x 50". *Hooked by Shirley G. Evans.*

Cora Feintuch

The technique of hooking lends itself not only to rugs but also to other useful and decorative objects such as bags and pouches. Pattern makers unknown. Hooked by Cora Feintuch. Tennessee. 2000. 15" x 15" and 7" x 9". *Courtesy of Cora Feintuch.*

A vibrant kaleidoscopic design makes for a handsome hooked rug. "Chinese Roundel." Designed by Jane McGown Flynn. House of Price / Charco pattern. Hooked by Cora Feintuch. Tennessee. 2006. Diameter 36". *Courtesy of Cora Feintuch.*

"Monkeys and Wild Cats" was inspired by favorite wallpaper. A band of leopard spots, edged in "tiger" orange, connects clusters of jungle foliage. Hooked by Cora Feintuch. Tennessee. 2003. 23.5" x 33". *Courtesy of Cora Feintuch.*

Utilizing a limited color palette, the bold stylized floral and leaf designs of "Tuesday" float upon light and dark fields. I look forward to "Wednesday." Designed by M. Hoops. Hooked by Cora Feintuch. Tennessee. 2007. 30" x 54". *Courtesy of Cora Feintuch.*

Richard Lee Scott

Reminiscent of a French impressionistic painting, a subtly changing scroll border complements a bouquet of "Spring Time" flowers, including pansies, daffodils, iris, tulips, and bleeding heart. Hooking since 1988, Richard prefers to use strips of woolen fabric cut 3/32" wide when creating his rugs. The finer the cut of wool, the finer the detail one can realize. Living in Georgia, Richard often travels to Chattanooga to meet with fellow hooking artists. Designed by Joan Moshimer. W. Cushing and Company pattern. Hooked by Richard Lee Scott. Georgia. 2008. 28" x 46". *Courtesy of Richard Lee Scott.*

AND THEN THERE IS CHARLOTTE…

Charlotte Gray

"I have hooked for ten years with the same group of ten women. I love colors, textures, and choices in rug hooking. Rug camps and teachers enrich the hooking experience. You learn constantly. The friends you meet are priceless." "Christmas Whimsy" incorporates bright happy colors that "show your personality through art." Designed and hooked by Charlotte Gray. Tennessee. 2007. 24" x 18". *Courtesy of Charlotte Gray.*

Charlotte Vandergriff

"I am one of ten women who have been meeting every Monday night for ten years. Our hooked work is as varied as we are – our bond is priceless." "Charlotte's Girls." Inspired by an e-mail image. Hooked by Charlotte Vandergriff. Tennessee. 2008. 18" x 20". *Courtesy of Charlotte Vandergriff.*

Chapter 5

GEORGIA On My Mind

From the venerable old homes of Savannah to the beltway and towering glass structures of Atlanta, Georgia is a state full of wondrous contrast. From mountain ranges to the Atlantic shore, the climate is warm and so are the people. Laying claim to a proud Southern heritage, the "Peach Tree State" is also home to a growing population of rug hooking artists.

Diane Chipman

An exquisitely executed hooked still life of "Tulips" was Diane Chipman's first attempt at realistic shading. She used strips of woolen fabric cut 3/32" wide to create an interesting stage for her flowers and foliage. "I wanted a subtle background of fern fronds. To me, hooking is almost a meditative experience." Adapted from a watercolor painting. Hooked by Diane Chipman. Georgia. 2007. 26" x 30". *Courtesy of Diane Chipman.*

"Baa Baa Baa Sheep." "I just wanted to do a 'funky' sheep rug that looked like wooly wiggles but was hooked 'flat' so it could be on the floor." Inspired by a wall plaque. Hooked by Diane Chipman. Georgia. 2005. 25" x 26". *Courtesy of Diane Chipman.*

Under full sail against a painted sky, the "Flying Cloud" cuts through rough seas. Hooked as a gift for Diane Chipman's daughter-in-law who chose the pattern and commissioned the pattern maker Jane Olson of California to specially hand-dye the woolen fabrics for the project. Designed by Jane Olson. Hooked by Diane Chipman. Georgia. 2008. 24" x 30". *Courtesy of Diane Chipman.*

WIREGRASS RUG HOOKERS GUILD
Thomasville, Georgia

The Wiregrass Rug Hookers Guild, formed in 2003, is named for the native grass that beautifies and preserves the soil of Georgia and adjacent states. Boasting twenty-five members in both Georgia and Florida, the 100th chapter of ATHA (Association of Traditional Hooking Artists) meets every Monday at the Thomas County Library in Thomasville.

Members are encouraged to try all forms of hooking such as fine shading, pictorials, stained glass, and primitive. They do not limit themselves to any particular style or technique. What follows is a sampling of their hooked work including an early source of inspiration.

Zorayda Sheets Bussom

"Julia Ann" was a present for a very special Georgia granddaughter born under the zodiac sign of Cancer. The sun shines down on the family's black and white dog, a puppy pal and nut-munching squirrel. Designed and hooked Zorayda Sheets Bussom. Ohio. 1971. 48" x 29". *Courtesy of Jane Bussom.*

Designed by 80-year-old life long rug hooker, Zorayda Sheets Bussom, "What To Do" glamorizes the queen of the throne and all that encompasses her bathroom kingdom. A royal banner of TP frames the sovereign ruler of curlers, creams, and air-drying nylons. "My mother-in-law hooked with a group of women in Shelby, Ohio. During the 1950s, a hooking instructor who lived in Cleveland would make weekly trips by train to teach. My interest in rug hooking developed while watching Zorayda hook her rugs. 'What To Do' now hangs in my workroom in Georgia where I enjoy it daily." Designed and hooked by Zorayda Sheets Bussom. Ohio. 1980. 62" x 34". *Courtesy of Jane Bussom*

Jane Bussom

"Twin Hearts." "The name is confusing since I omitted the two hearts from the design. I added another star and the date." Skillfully, Jane melds the colors and elements of crewelwork embroidery with Pennsylvania Dutch motifs. Designed by Joan Moshimer. W. Cushing and Company pattern. Hooked by Jane Bussom. Georgia. 2007. 32" x 54". *Courtesy of Jane Bussom.*

Bettye Day Adams

The "19th Hole" was hooked as a birthday gift for a husband that played golf for the University of Georgia, hence the "G" on his attire. Designed by Beverly Conway. Hooked by Bettye Day Adams. Georgia. 2008. 52" x 28". *Courtesy of Bettye Day Adams.*

Susan Arthur

Rug hookers are a talented and well-traveled lot. Susan Arthur lives in Florida, belongs to the Wiregrass Rug Hookers Guild in Georgia and chose to hook a Maine "Lobsterman." The late Joan Moshimer, a New Zealand artist, who as a war bride came to the United States and settled with her husband in Kennebunkport, Maine, designed the pattern. Susan used her wool strips to paint this coastal inspired scene. The day is done and the colors of the setting sun are reflected on Atlantic waters. W. Cushing and Company pattern. Hooked by Susan Arthur. Florida. 2007. 26" x 44". *Courtesy of Susan Arthur*.

Now that's the way to deal with bills! "Goat Mail." Jacqueline Hansen Designs. Hooked by Susan Arthur. Florida. 2007. 25" x 37". *Courtesy of Susan Arthur.*

Wyatt Nocera

"This started out as an 'Apple Tree' design donated to our guild. I needed to practice hooking curves and wanted to work with colors outside my comfort zone…thus modern flowers." The hooked piece became a decorative covering for a footstool. Pattern maker unknown. Hooked by Wyatt Nocera. Georgia. 2007. Diameter 18". *Courtesy of Wyatt Nocera*.

There is nothing like sitting and watching the world go by from your rocking chair and "Home is Where the Heart Is" makes that sitting a bit more comfortable. This hooked chair pad utilizes both solid and plaid woolen fabrics. Designed and hooked by Wyatt Nocera. Georgia. 2006. 16" x 15". *Courtesy of Wyatt Nocera*.

Amanda Burroughs

"Turdunkin" is a bird-like creature doodled by a friend in art class. "When flipping through her drawings I had to hook this bird." Designed by Cissie DeMott. Hooked by Amanda Burroughs. Georgia. 2008. 11" x 18". *Courtesy of Amanda Burroughs.*

Patricia Byrd

Rug hookers embrace a green world and love to re-cycle. When hooking her "Fox and Grapes" rug, Pat Byrd used a Goodwill store skirt for the grapes and gifted green wools for the leaves. Edyth O'Neill Design. Hooked by Patricia Byrd. Georgia. 2007. 31.5" x 40.5". *Courtesy of Patricia M. Byrd.*

Dona Carruth

"'Dragon Fly Dreaming' is my first attempt at rug hooking." Warm summer breezes blow across a pond and propel this colorful winged messenger along its way. Designed and hooked by Dona Carruth. Georgia. 2008. 22" x 22". *Courtesy of Dona Carruth.*

Charity Rojas

"I am in my 30s and in love with fiber. I am a hooker, spinner, and weaver. And a close friend, knowing I like 'Celtic' designs, gave me this pattern." Harry M. Fraser and Co. pattern. Hooked by Charity Rojas. Georgia. 2007. 11" x 13.5". *Courtesy of Charity Rojas of Charity's Creations.*

Larayne Cunningham

"While living in the Washington, D.C., area, I attended a county fair and saw the work of a local hooking teacher and her students. I signed up for my first rug class in 1981 and have been hooked ever since. We retired in South Georgia and I was delighted to find the Wiregrass Rug Hookers who meet in Thomasville." Pictured is a detail of "My Mac." Inspiration for the hooked portrait came from a small photo of Larayne Cunningham's four-year-old granddaughter. Hooked by Larayne Cunningham. Georgia. 2008. Finished size 47" x 37". *Courtesy of Larayne Cunningham.*

Each year members of the Wiregrass Rug Hookers Guild donate their time and talents and create a rug for charity. Raffle tickets are sold with proceeds benefiting the Thomas County food bank. The drawing for the rug is held in conjunction with the group's annual exhibit at the local library. Georgia. 2008. *Courtesy of the Wiregrass Rug Hookers Guild.*

Becky Jackson

Gardening and Hooking Bring Comfort

"Since I love growing hydrangeas in my yard, I decided to hook one to enjoy inside my home." An avid gardener and a needlepoint artist Becky Jackson combined traditional hooking with "proddy" work. She then added embroidered French knots to produce a three-dimensional "Hydrangea" blossom pillow. Designed and hooked by Becky Jackson. Georgia. 2008. 18" x 18". *Courtesy of Becky Jackson.*

ERIC SANDBERG
Athens, Georgia

After almost thirty years and forty motion pictures, Eric Sandberg retired from the film industry and left Hollywood in 2000 to become a full time rug hooking teacher. Eventually he relocated to Athens, Georgia.

Besides teaching monthly classes in his home, he travels regularly to rug camps and workshops throughout the United States. He is also the director of the popular Caraway Rug School held annually in Asheboro, North Carolina. The photos shown here are the bulk of his work of fifteen years. Even with his busy schedule, Eric tries to complete one rug a year. You may also find him seated as a student in one of your classes at rug camp… as he is a firm believer in continuing education.

Photos courtesy of Roy Schwen.

Georgia hooking artist and teacher Eric Sandberg poses with a student attending a much-anticipated workshop he conducted in Crossville, Tennessee. 2008. *Courtesy of By Hook or By Crook.*

Utilizing his "snarl" bag of narrow and wide pre-cut odds and ends, Eric Sandberg hooked "Paisley Stair Tread." "This is a great piece for a workshop on color and using scraps." Harry M. Fraser Co. pattern. Hooked by Eric Sandberg. Georgia. 2002. 10" x 18". *Courtesy of Eric H. Sandberg.*

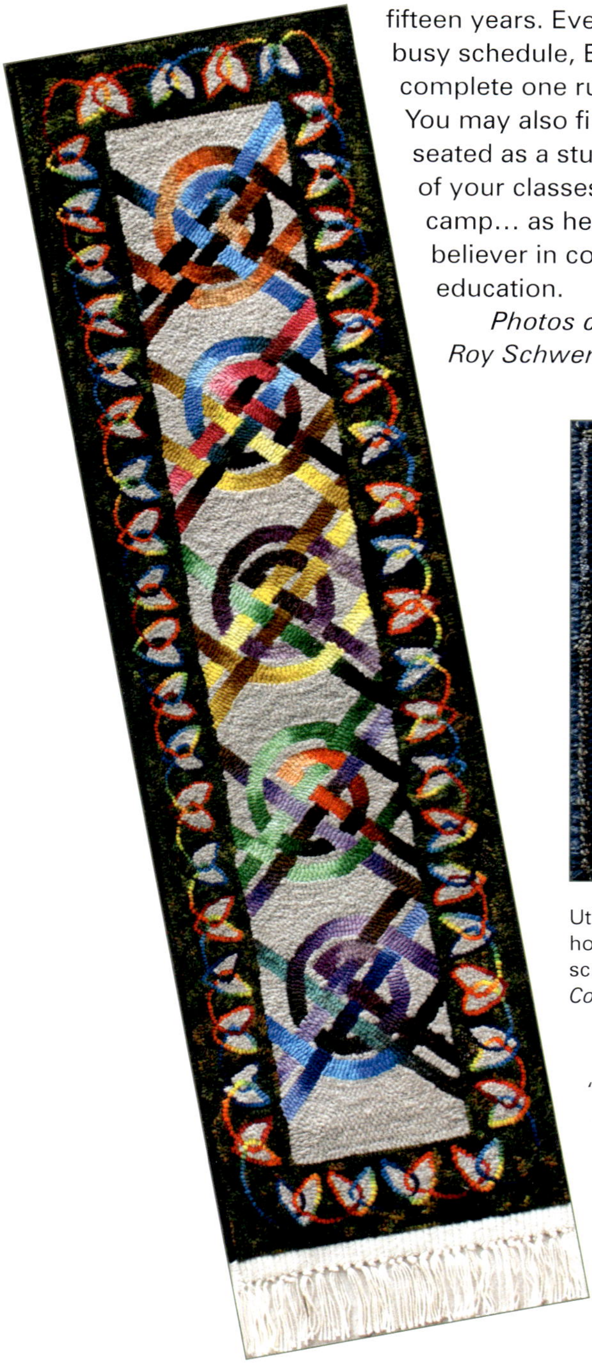

"Celtic Knots" exemplifies the use of "light, bright, dark, and dull" to create an aesthetically pleasing hooked work of art. Each of the knots displays a different color harmony. Designed by Jane McGown Flynn. Hooked by Eric Sandberg. Georgia. 2008. 48" x 13". *Courtesy of Eric H. Sandberg.*

Too many patterns, not enough time. "Prudence" was never finished and has been sold "as is." Originally hooked with a primary color harmony of red, yellow, and blue, it is Eric's hope that the new owner will complete the project. Pearl McGown pattern. Hooked by Eric Sandberg. Georgia. A work in progress. 37"x 30". *Courtesy of Eric H. Sandberg*.

"Africa's Gift." "One of my favorite rugs. I commissioned Jane Flynn to design a geranium rug that had a masculine feel to it. I did this rug under the tutelage of rug hooking teacher, Ramona Maddox. Each leaf is different. Notice that the flowers are brighter in the upper left corner, implying a light source. This is my first rug for which I did all the dyeing." Designed by Jane McGown Flynn. Hooked by Eric Sandberg. Georgia. 1998. 29" x 42". *Courtesy of Eric H. Sandberg.*

"Polish Wedding Rug" was designed and hooked for Eric's goddaughter, Christie. She and her husband stood on the treasured heirloom when they took their vows. Designed and hooked by Eric Sandberg. (The pattern is available from House of Price / Charco.) Georgia. 2007. 16" x 42". *Courtesy of Eric H. Sandberg.*

Eric gives personal attention to a By Hook or By Crook student attending his workshop. Tennessee. 2008. *Courtesy of By Hook or By Crook.*

Limiting himself to using only tweeds from his famous "snarl bag" of odds and ends, Eric crafted "Stars, Stars, Stars." The overall effect reminds one of a crazy quilt, in design, color, and variety of textures. Adaptation of an antique rug. Woolley Fox pattern. Hooked by Eric Sandberg. Georgia. 2007. 27" x 34". *Courtesy of Eric H. Sandberg.*

As a certified McGown instructor, "Sarah" was the first rug Eric was assigned to teach at The McGown Teachers' Workshop held in Eugene, Oregon during 1997. His goal was to hook a rug with yellow flowers that were not harsh or garish. Designed by Jane McGown Flynn. House of Price / Charco pattern. Hooked by Eric Sandberg. Georgia. 2000. 24" x 36". *Courtesy of Eric H. Sandberg.*

"'Metamorphosis' was my first rug. I didn't have a teacher yet and followed instructions from a five part series in *Rug Hooking* magazine authored by Jane Flynn." Designed by Jane McGown Flynn. House of Price / Charco pattern. Hooked by Eric Sandberg. Georgia. 1994. 19" x 30". *Courtesy of Eric H. Sandberg.*

Eric's faithful and always handy "snarl bag" provided the pre-cut odd and end strips to hook "Duncan." "I have taught this rug many times and it comes out different every time, depending on the leftover stash brought by students." Pearl McGown pattern. Hooked by Eric Sandberg. Georgia. 2003. 25" x 37". *Courtesy of Eric H. Sandberg.*

"Hooking instructions for 'Easter Parade' are described in great detail in Vera Bisbee Underhill's 1951 *Creating Hooked Rugs*. I was going away on location for six months to Philadelphia and Baltimore to work on the movie "12 Monkeys" (1995) and had no rug hooking teacher. Following the instructions in the book made this rug, my second, easy and the results are beautiful. Almost half done, it's rolled up under the bed, probably never to be finished." (A note from the author: Hollywood may have lost one of its best costumer supervisors but the rug hooking world gained one of its greatest hooking artists.) Designed by Louise Zeiser. Heirloom Rugs pattern. Hooked by Eric Sandberg. Georgia. Unfinished. 64" x 37". *Courtesy of Eric H. Sandberg.*

"Spanish Repeat" uses up scraps and allows you to "play" with color. Designed and hooked by Eric Sandberg. Georgia. 2006. 16" x 20". *Courtesy of Eric H. Sandberg*.

"Le Chateau" is by far Eric's most famous work, earning him a place of honor among the Who's Who of the rug hooking world. "A step by step explanation of this piece and the technique I developed was featured in an article I wrote for *Rug Hooking* magazine in 2003." The favorite of many and recipient of several awards, "Le Chateau" was entirely hooked upside down; an unusual technique that Eric developed and perfected. Hooking students clamor to learn his "Castle Technique." Adapted from a 19th century French painting. Charco pattern. Hooked by Eric Sandberg. Georgia. 1999. 17" x 22". *Courtesy of Eric H. Sandberg.*

"'Mini Prudence,' one of my favorite pieces, was hooked in a couple of days. The background space between the diamonds is dull to offset the light, bright and dark diamond shapes." Adapted from a Pearl McGown pattern. Hooked by Eric Sandberg. Georgia. 2007. 6" x 10". *Courtesy of Eric H. Sandberg*.

"Using hand-dyed woolen fabrics that gradually transition from light to dark made 'Second Thought' very easy to hook." Designed by Jane McGown Flynn. House of Price / Charco pattern. Hooked by Eric Sandberg. Georgia. 2006. 21" x 36". *Courtesy of Eric H. Sandberg.*

"Turkish Primitive" was hooked with hand-dyed wools of red, blue and yellow; all else came from Eric's "snarl bag" of pre-cut odds and ends. Designed by Jane McGown Flynn. House of Price / Charco pattern. Hooked by Eric Sandberg. Georgia. 2007. 32" x 56". *Courtesy of Eric H. Sandberg.*

Relying on his trusty "snarl bag," Eric fashioned his adaptation of "First Thought." Designed by Jane McGown Flynn. House of Price / Charco pattern. Hooked by Eric Sandberg. Georgia. 2001. 16" x 24". *Courtesy of Eric H. Sandberg.*

"Flock." "This piece was very inspiring. Designed and hooked in less than a week, once again I used my 'Castle Technique' and hooked the entire piece upside down. I left the background unhooked for a more dramatic effect." Designed and hooked by Eric Sandberg. Georgia. 2007. 18" x 36". *Courtesy of Eric H. Sandberg.*

A GALLERY OF MORE GEORGIA HOOKING ARTISTS

Beth Gibbs

"I began hooking after starting chemo treatments for non-Hodgkin's lymphoma. My sister, who was already a hooker, taught me how to get my mind off what I was going through. It worked and I loved hooking, dyeing, and designing rugs. I saw the pattern for 'The Old Pot' and had to hook it." Designed by M. Hoops Fleetwood. Hooked by Beth Gibbs. Georgia. 2005. 27" x 38". *Courtesy of Beth Gibbs*.

"I do a lot of my own designing, color planning, and dyeing and love to use recycled wool in my rugs. Most of my work is given as gifts to those I love. The design and color plan of 'Santa Fe Comfort' was worked over the Internet with Kim Nixon. She's awesome!" And so are her stools. (Kim Nixon's hooked stools are showcased in the Tennessee chapter.) Designed by Kim Nixon and Beth Gibbs. Hooked by Beth Gibbs. Georgia. 2006. 12" x 16". *Courtesy of Beth Gibbs*.

"I hooked as a child with my 'Big Mom.' She was my mother's best friend who lived on a farm where I would visit for two or three weeks at a time. Upstairs in a bedroom she worked on a large rug pulled taut on a big old frame. We would go into town and chose our wool from the Salvation Army and hand-cut it into hooking strips. After she passed away, I didn't pick up a hook again until I reached my 50s... I have not laid it down since." "Early Frost" was inspired by the "Turkish" hooked rug patterns designed by Edward Sands Frost of Maine in the late 1800s. Designed by Kay Forbush. Hooked by Sandy Myers. Georgia. 2004. 22" x 42". *Courtesy of Sandy Myers.*

"I am fascinated with the history of Edward Sands Frost, the Maine tin peddler who designed rug patterns in the late 1800s." "Frost Oriental" was hooked using #4, #5, and #6 cut strips of wool – 4/32", 5/32", and 6/32". Designed by Edward Sands Frost. W. Cushing and Company pattern. Hooked by Sandy Myers. Georgia. 2007. 38" x 76". *Courtesy of Sandy Myers.*

Joan Payton

The Bishop of Atlanta commissioned Joan Payton to hook "Compass Rose" for the Episcopal Diocesan office. Each point of the compass represents a human race in the world of Anglican churches. Designed and hooked by Joan Payton. Georgia. 2008. 4′ x4′. *Courtesy of Joan Payton.*

"I made 'Eggs and Bacon' for my first grandchild Margaret Cross Payton. It hangs in her room and adds lots of fun and color." Pris Buttler Design. Hooked by Joan Payton. Georgia. 2008. 29″ x 38″. *Courtesy of Joan Payton*.

"Glory to God in the Highest" is a hooked memorial tribute for Etta Taylor Coyne honoring her many years of ministry to Children of the Cathedral. It hangs in the Children's Chapel, Cathedral of St. Philip in Atlanta, Georgia. Designed and hooked by Joan Payton. Georgia. 2007. 3.5′ x 6′. *Courtesy of Joan Payton.*

Becky Vickery

"I enjoyed hooking 'Secret Garden Revisited' in my 'sophisticated primitive style'. A needle was put in my hand by my grandmother at the age of five years old. I have enjoyed various needlecrafts over the years. Ten years ago I found a love and an art form in rug hooking." Karen Kahle / Primitive Spirit pattern. Hooked by Becky Vickery. Georgia. 2006. 31" x 50". *Courtesy of Becky Vickery.*

"Designer Pris Buttler was gracious to alter 'Best Friends' in order to make the pattern more personal. Each girl represents my daughters who are best friends. They are depicted holding their own pets with our dog Darby 'pouting' in the background. A likeness of my mother's handwriting was used for the verse. My grandfather's apple grafting skills made it alright for the apples on the tree to be all different." Designed by Pris Buttler. Hooked by Becky Vickery. Georgia. 2001. 35" x 43". *Courtesy of Becky Vickery.*

A Jacobean embroidery motif meets Georgia O'Keefe. "I loved the dimensions of the single floral design in 'Little Crewe.' This was a fun piece to hook." Designed by Patsy Becker. Hooked by Becky Vickery. Georgia. 2003. 24" x 36". *Courtesy of Becky Vickery.*

Linda Christman

"To fully appreciate 'Lindsay's Sheep and Bears' you need to understand its story. My father, a stained glass artisan, created a sheep and teddy bear piece with my daughter in 1985. And though he passed in 1991, his spirit is still a driving force in the family. When it was time to create a custom rug for my granddaughter and namesake, Lindsay, there was no question that her great-grandpa's sheep and bear would be the basis of the design. I wanted to incorporate a surprise so I added a small bunny smelling a flower. This rug binds four generations of my family together." Designed and hooked by Linda Christman. Georgia. 2008. Diameter 36". *Courtesy of Linda A. Christman.*

"Shooting Stars" was inspired by a quilt square design. "I dye my own wool with reclaimed water using various dyeing techniques including casserole, jar, trans-color, marbleizing and spot." Designed and hooked by Linda Christman. Georgia. 2007. 15" x 50". *Courtesy of Linda A. Christman.*

JOAN McCLUNG
Atlanta, Georgia

An active long-time member and past president of the Atlanta's Dogwood Chapter of ATHA (Association of Traditional Hooking Artists), Joan McClung's hooking career focuses on wide cut primitive patterns.

"The flowers of 'Welcome Mat' were my first experience with dyeing. The letters were hooked from a re-cycled skirt and the background from an 'as is' uniform." Pattern maker unknown. Hooked by Joan McClung. Virginia. 1952. 13" x 34". *Courtesy of Joan McClung.*

Pictured in front of her favorite magnolia tree, hooking artist Joan McClung, works on one of her many rug hooking projects. "I began hooking in 1951. My husband was in the navy, stationed in Arlington, Virginia. We had a small apartment and a small child. I learned to hook using books from the local library. I had never seen a hooked rug before. I had very few pieces of wool and almost no patterns were available." Georgia. 2008. *Courtesy of Joan McClung.*

"Poppies," another early rug hooking project. Pattern maker unknown. Hooked by Joan McClung. Virginia. 1952. 20" x 53". *Courtesy of Joan McClung.*

For several years Joan's hooking talents were put on hold while she pursued a career in the banking industry. In 1990 she once again picked up her hook and hasn't put it down since. Pictured is a detail from her "Houses and Churches" rug. "My hooking career focuses on primitive patterns that use wide cut strips." Barbara Brown pattern. Hooked by Joan McClung. Georgia. 1990. Finished rug size 20" x 41". *Courtesy of Joan McClung.*

Originally of New England origins, "Sailcloth Primitive" is a favorite pattern hooked by many rug makers throughout the United States and Canada. Heirloom Rugs pattern. Hooked by Joan McClung. Georgia. 1995. 29" x 68". *Courtesy of Joan McClung*.

Detail of "Sailcloth Primitive." *Courtesy of Joan McClung.*

Attracted to "Scalloped Fantasy," Joan McClung had the designer make the pattern into a long hall runner. Pictured is a small portion of the lengthy project. Designed by Janet Carija Brandt. Hooked by Joan McClung. Georgia. 1995. 11.5' x 30". *Courtesy of Joan McClung.*

Detail of "Scalloped Fantasy." *Courtesy of Joan McClung*.

Pictured is a detail of "Power Leap Farm," located in a little town just north of Atlanta. Stopping by her daughter's farm one Sunday afternoon, Joan McClung and her husband found the whole family planting flowers beside the driveway. The memorable scene made such an impression that Joan was inspired to hook this rug. Designed and hooked by Joan McClung. Georgia. 1996. Finished rug size 34" x 46". *Courtesy of Joan McClung.*

"I Sing Behind the Plow" was adapted from the John C. Campbell Folk School logo. Founded in 1925, the North Carolina school was an "alternative to the higher education facilities that drew intelligent young people away from family farms." Today the school embraces a rich history of hands on instruction and lists rug hooking among their many offered courses. Joan Payton's hooked tribute to hard work features silhouetted figures and inspirational words. Hooked by Joan McClung. Georgia. 1999. 17" x 24". *Courtesy of Joan McClung.*

"Sunflowers" reach for the sky and venture outside a confining border. Pattern maker unknown. Hooked by Joan McClung. Georgia. 1999. 53" x 30". *Courtesy of Joan McClung.*

Under a night sky this productive "Hen," toting a full basket of eggs, struts back to her Southern home. "The flag was changed to that of the Confederate states." Lib Callaway patterns. Hooked by Joan McClung. Georgia. 1999. 26" x 36". *Courtesy of Joan McClung.*

After long admiring the repetitive paisley design of "Persian Palm," Joan McClung hooked the popular pattern for herself. Heirloom Rugs pattern. Hooked by Joan McClung. Georgia. 2006. 37" x 68". *Courtesy of Joan McClung*.

Detail of "Persian Palm." *Courtesy of Joan McClung.*

JOY VANNERSON – PERSONAL MEMORIES

I began rug hooking with Mary Paul Wright and a group of delightful hookers in 2000 At the time I was living in my cabin, which was moved by our family from the middle of Georgia and restored on the shore of Lake Lanier, about an hour north of Atlanta. It is a double-pen, story-and-a-half log home built around the time of the Civil War from hand hewn heart pine logs.

My hooking project of "A Series of Four Personal Memories" seemed perfect for the cabin and was planned for display on the extra tall risers of the very steep stairs that lead to the upstairs bedrooms. My plan was to depict different personal and family memories on each stair riser.

I then moved back to our Atlanta home that has shorter risers that didn't fit my hooking, and I decided to make my hooked pieces into pillows. Three of the pieces depict the only three homes where I have ever lived. The fourth is my daughter on her first horse.

I still have visions of other memories to hook... my children at the beach, my son and husband in boats, special friends, our most memorable cat and dog... and others... that I hope to do some day.

I am intrigued with subject matter that is personally important, and find it satisfying, engaging, and therapeutic to select and design with the existing colors of "gizzards" (leftover or discarded wool strips) and small pieces of wool.

"A Series of Personal Memories" depicts from top to bottom "Lake Lanier Cabin," "Dunwoody House," "Wendy on Cheerio" and "Miami Home." "'Lake Lanier Cabin,' the first in the series, has sheltered families since the mid-nineteenth century and it is still our family's warm and personable lake cabin. 'Dunwoody House' depicts my family's primary home for the last 40 years, where my children were raised and where I still live. Most of my adult memories reside here. I considered selling it following the death of my husband, but discovered it was the only place I found myself 'singing out loud.' 'Wendy on Cheerio' is my daughter on her first horse. The design was based on a horse show photo. Cheerio went with my daughter to Berry College in North Georgia where she studied animal science. Wendy is now a professional equestrian, training horses and coaching students in Alpharetta, Georgia. 'Miami House' is the home where I grew up and lived before going away to college. The smaller home to the left is the home of my paternal grandparents and my great-aunt Minnie. Alligators actually lived in the canal, but the flamingo is a bit of artistic license. These Miami homes were filled with sunshine and love, but exist now only in the fond memories of my sister and me and very few others." Designed and hooked by Joy Vannerson. Georgia. 2008. Each hooked piece is 8.5" x 24". *Courtesy of Joy Vannerson.*

AND MORE GEORGIA HOOKING ARTISTS

Elizabeth Rowe

Elephants, magic carpets, peacocks, horses and noblemen tell the tales of ancient India. An edging of eight-petal flowers frames "Kashani Hunt." Designed by Jane McGown Flynn. House of Price / Charco pattern. Hooked by Elizabeth Rowe. Georgia. 2003. 73" x 43". *Courtesy of Elizabeth Rowe.*

Swirling about in an imaginary wind, delicately shaded Jacobean-like flowers radiate out from a central floral medallion. A three-year project, "Kashan Fantasy" has always been a favorite of hooking artist, Elizabeth Rowe. Pearl McGown pattern. Hooked by Elizabeth Rowe. Georgia. 1977. 46" x 83". *Courtesy of Elizabeth Rowe.*

Inspired by a late 17th century Chinese design, "Peony Hedge" combines angular architectural details with the flowing curves of flowers and foliage. This Chinoiserie pattern was shortened because "I got tired of hooking peonies!" Pearl McGown pattern. Hooked by Elizabeth Rowe. Georgia. 1982. 51" x 67". *Courtesy of Elizabeth Rowe.*

"Slav" combines rustic East European folk art figures with geometric patterns. Pearl McGown pattern. Hooked by Elizabeth Rowe. Georgia. 2001. 47" x 32". Courtesy of *Elizabeth Rowe.*

Rich tones of gold and moss green set the stage for jewel-like touches of color. An appealing hooked Persian-style rug "Sheik," recalls its proud heritage. Pearl McGown pattern. Hooked by Elizabeth Rowe. Georgia. 1974. 32" x 50". *Courtesy of Elizabeth Rowe.*

Sporting stylized diamond medallions of a colorful lot "Prudence" adds a note of cheer to any décor. Pearl McGown pattern. Hooked by Elizabeth Rowe. Georgia. 2004. 32" x 48". *Courtesy of Elizabeth Rowe.*

Five diminutive flowers, lined up in a row and placed in a large goblet-like urn are protected by a pink dome of color. Spindly flower stalks flank the centerpiece. This naïve hooked and framed folk art study recalls, in design and color, Victorian mourning images. "Amherst Floral." Black Sheep Wool Designs. Hooked by Nancy Fuchs. Georgia. 2000. 30.5" x 35". *Courtesy of Nancy Fuchs*.

"Cats in Padulas." Felines in fanciful flowers; an amusing place to rest one's head. Pris Buttler Rug Designs. Hooked by Nancy Fuchs. Georgia. 2007. 16" x 16.5". *Courtesy of Nancy Fuchs*.

Hovering around the queen. "Bees Knee" hooked pillow. Pris Buttler Rug Designs. Hooked by Nancy Fuchs. Georgia. 2007. 16" x 16.5". *Courtesy of Nancy Fuchs.*

A trio of posies and tulips and forget-me-not sprays by the pair – all symmetrically balanced – spring forth from a vase of sturdy proportions. Untitled. Designed by Diane Stoffel. Hooked by Nancy Fuchs. Georgia. 2006. 22" x 19.5". *Courtesy of Nancy Fuchs.*

Chris Preble

A hooked portrait panel of the "Five Preble Kitties" immortalizes furry family members. Designed by Elizabeth Black. Hooked by Chris Preble. Georgia. 2008. 57" x 15". *Courtesy of Chris Preble.*

Combining the likeness of a wedding gift with her hooking and newly learned prodding skills, Chris Preble presented "Wedding Crock Bouquet" to her son and his new wife. Designed and hooked by Chris Preble. Georgia. 2007. 24.5" x 19.5" *Courtesy of Chris Preble.*

Elaine Zimney

A red roofed home of narrow dimensions is dwarfed by a magical "Towne Garden." Open the gate and love pours out. A saw-tooth border frames the whimsical scene. "My first rug!" Karen Kahle / Primitive Spirit pattern. Hooked by Elaine Zimney. Georgia. 2005. 32" x 31". *Courtesy of Elaine Zimney.*

Lollypop flowers guard a large stylized tulip on "Hadley Welcom." Of early American design, hooking artist Elaine Zimney modified the pattern by leaving off the old world "Welcom" greeting. Edyth O'Neill Design. Hooked by Elaine Zimney. Georgia. 2005. 21" x 36". *Courtesy of Elaine Zimney.*

"Antique Rose Runner" features a trio of bloom and bud filled diamonds resting on a field of hit or miss stripes. Karen Kahle / Primitive Spirit pattern. Hooked by Elaine Zimney. Georgia. 2006. 21" x 53". *Courtesy of Elaine Zimney.*

Posed on a bed of fanciful flowers, this folk art king of the beasts sports a toothy grin and "wobbly" legs. "Antique Lion." Karen Kahle / Primitive Spirit pattern. Hooked by Elaine Zimney. Georgia. 2005. 26" x 51". *Courtesy of Elaine Zimney.*

Growing in a scalloped bed of hooked earth, floating roses hover above and around an unused garden trellis. "Moss Rose." Karen Kahle / Primitive Spirit pattern. Hooked by Elaine Zimney. Georgia. 2005. 23" x 34". *Courtesy of Elaine Zimney.*

A rug to be enjoyed from all angles; imaginary flowering trees sprout up from the sidewalks of a whimsical "Flowerbox" village. Karen Kahle / Primitive Spirit pattern. Hooked by Elaine Zimney. Georgia. 2005. 24" x 36". *Courtesy of Elaine Zimney.*

A work in progress. "'Country Cottage' was modified to look like my cottage on Lake Lanier in Cumming, Georgia. In November 2004 I started hooking with a passion." Rug Wool Studio pattern. Hooked by Elaine Zimney. Georgia. 2008. 40" x 46". *Courtesy of Elaine Zimney*.

Susan DiPuma

Paisley motifs frame a patch of hooked posies. "Heart-Shaped Stool." Designed and hooked by Susan DiPuma. Georgia. 2008. 8.5" x 12". *Courtesy of Susan DiPuma*

A relaxing place for both feet and birds; an abstract sky is the backdrop for two cardinals resting on a snow covered evergreen branch. "Cardinals' Stool." Adapted from a pattern by Jane Olson in *The Rug Hooker's Bible.* Hooked by Susan DiPuma. Georgia. 2008. 12" x 18". *Courtesy of Susan DiPuma.*

This old unsigned tile, a flea market find, inspired Susan DiPuma to create her own hooked "White Owl." Hooked by Susan DiPuma. Georgia. 2007. 31" x 31". *Courtesy of Susan DiPuma.*

Lita McCormick

"This pattern was part of a friend's 'stash' that came to me after she passed away. I wanted to hook it because she was intending to hook it. Every time I see it I think of her." A rustic twig frame, complete with a floral vine, contains an unlikely pair of "Dog and Deer." Pattern maker unknown. Hooked by Lita McCormick. Georgia. 2006. 46" x 54". *Courtesy of Lita McCormick.*

"'Whiskers' is our precious cat that crossed the road to come live with us. His old family misses him but he is ours now. I collected his whiskers over the years and used them in this rug." In addition to hooking with strips of woolen fabric and whiskers, angora yarns were used. Designed and hooked by Lita McCormick. Georgia. 2006. 29" x 27". *Courtesy of Lita McCormick.*

"Olivia," a fuzzy little ostrich chick, was hooked from woolen fabrics, yarns, and feathers. Designed by Elizabeth Black. Hooked by Lita McCormick. Georgia. 2007. 23" x 18". *Courtesy of Lita McCormick.*

SUZANNE HOLTKAMP
Buford, Georgia

If the late Tasha Tudor had a young Southern clone, it would be Suzanne Holtkamp. Suzanne embraces a pure and simple life and approaches rug hooking with a passion seen by few. She is a true hooking artist; an avid researcher of all things hooked and has become an absolutely delightful friend.

Photographs of individual rugs were taken by Blane Marable / Blane Marable Photography, Athens, Georgia. "Lifestyle" photographs were taken by Beverly Goodrich and Suzanne Holtkamp."

Suzanne Holtkamp's little piece of hooking paradise. "Sometimes it's hard to know when the rug studio ends and the garden begins. I like it that way." Georgia. 2008. *Courtesy of Suzanne Holtkamp.*

My Rug Hooking Story

It's kind of curious how I began hooking. I have always been an artistic sort, dabbling in everything from watercolor painting to pastels to knitting and sewing. I can never remember a time in my life when I didn't have some sort of artistic endeavor going, but I never really latched onto any one of the mediums in particular.

After the birth of my second child in 1999, I found myself home a lot with a touch of postpartum depression. Even though I was still an active part of the business my husband and I had begun some four years earlier, I found myself getting restless. By chance one day, I happened upon a craft show that portrayed a New England woman and her rug hooking studio. (I don't remember the name of the hooker, but I am sure that if I heard her name now, I would know exactly who she is!) It intrigued me so much that I began looking for any book I could lay my hands on that would explain to me how to do this "hooking thing."

It just so happened that I bought a copy of Anne Mather's rug hooking book which detailed pages of wonderful women and their rugs. I devoured the book and many others. From these books, I taught myself to dye and turned my kitchen into a wool dyer's paradise. I shopped the thrift stores and dyed lots and lots of wool but was intimidated about actually using it in a rug.

Later that year, I came across a copy of *Rug Hooking* magazine in Michael's Craft Store while visiting my family in Ohio on vacation. In the back of the magazine, I noticed there was an ad for a hooking group in Athens, Georgia. I called this Nancy Thompson person and the rest is history. She invited me to a hook-in they were having. After arriving and being introduced around the room, I began to recognize names from my Mather book! I found out that Anne Mather was a member of the Atlanta Dogwood Guild right around the corner! I spent the rest of the afternoon gathering autographs and even though I now know these women very well, I still cherish that book, remembering my delight at meeting them and continue to be awed by their talent and insight.

Then came the natural dye thing. I had always been interested in the way rug hooking began in America and found myself drawn towards the earliest styles of hooking. Being an antiques lover, it was a natural fit. Eric Sandberg (Georgia rug hooking artist and teacher) twisted my arm (right?) into attending Caraway Rug School in North Carolina and it was during one of those camps that I met Nancy Blair who sold this wool called "Rusty Pot." I asked her how she did it and she said, "with a rusty pot!" Well, that wasn't good enough for me.

After camp, I began an intense search for anything that would show me how to dye wool naturally or as our ancestors would have called it, "vegetable dye." The books were all great for research but many of them contained directions for "stew pots with 150 gals of water and 5 lbs of aluminum." (Of course I am exaggerating, but not by much!) They were confusing nonetheless. As well, it seemed much of the natural dye information was still in use by other fiber artists like weavers and spinners but not so much rug hookers. When the student is ready, the teacher will appear.

Enter Jeanie Reagan, natural dyer, spinner, weaver, knitter, and owner of an historical homestead in Dahlonega, Georgia. I spent almost two years visiting Jeanie on "Wonderful Wednesdays" and enjoyed a great lively dialogue about native plants and natural dye techniques. She taught me about fibers, spinning, and weaving and helped me identify many native dye plants. I can only hope I taught her a little about hooking! I was able to adapt many of her dyeing techniques for hooking after a little trial and error. Hooking on her porch, watching her sheep in the meadow, with a dye pot steaming above the fire is a memory that will last me a lifetime.

Then came Jessie Turbayne to Caraway Rug Hooking School in North Carolina with her antique Frost #17 duck rug. (Have you noticed all these women whose names begin with J?) Well, that was the end of me again as I searched out everything I could find about Frost. That led me to Jane Radcliffe (J again) (guest curator of the 2004 Rugs All Marked Out Frost Exhibit) of the Maine State Museum. I volunteered to help Jane, via long-distance, with anything I could for the exhibit. I can't even begin to explain this wonderful time when I was privileged enough to work with her, get to know her, and help discover wonderful Frost facts. It truly was a great day when Jane would email, "Someone brought a Frost # (fill in the blank) and can you believe it had been in their mother's attic for at least 80 years?" Oh… the rush of a new find!

I have always loved trying new hooking styles and techniques, and purposely sign up for classes with teachers whom I have never had before. However, I find myself being drawn back to the origins of American rug hooking. I

If the late Tasha Tudor had a young Southern clone it would be Suzanne Holtkamp. Donning an historically accurate 1830s day dress, Suzanne gathers berries for her natural dyeing. "Pokeberries were used by Native Americans and pioneers alike." Georgia. 2008. *Courtesy of Suzanne Holtkamp*.

enjoy collecting antique rugs, studying them, and trying to identify vegetable dyes. This interest has led me to a host of wonderful people who always have interesting stories and fascinating opinions. I believe that seeking teachers outside the rug hooking world is very important as well. They often can solve a piece of the creative puzzle that comes from a different point of view.

My style reflects all these influences. I say this with love, but I know that my rugs have raised more than one eyebrow in hooking circles. I have been a thorn in many a rug hooking teacher's side because I don't like to follow the rules. Color plan? What's a color plan? Make sure you have enough wool for the whole rug before you start. Hello! Me have enough of one color? You may not turn under the edges and sew; that's simply not allowed. Okay, but that's what my grandmother did. Yes, I am going to try to do naturally dyed swatches. And by the way I hand cut most of my wool and am not shy about hooking double and clipping. Those are my dad's polyester plaid pants and somehow they're going to fit into this rug.

Dyeing for me is as much fun as hooking. Even though vegetable dyeing takes up to five times longer than chemically colored wool, it makes me feel close to our rug ancestors. And you know I am a sucker for hard work. I don't know what it is, but there's something about the exhaustion at the end of a really good dye day that just makes me feel as if I have accomplished something truly worthwhile. And the colors are ridiculously addictive. It doesn't hurt, either, that it combines my love of gardening. And I can dye outside with really big pots and gas tanks. What more could a girl ask for?

My future plans? At the present I have many UFOs (like most hookers) that I am insisting I will finish. I have a naturally dyed Waldoboro (raised and sculptured) rug that I began with Maine's Jacqueline Hansen, which will be the cat's meow when finished. (The authentic green Waldoboro color took me four weeks to figure out from vegetable dyes and you know what they say – I can give you the secret but then....) Fine shading artist Sybil Osicka from Ohio withstood my defiance as she helped me work with naturally dyed swatches in an Oriental-style rug. And then there's the double hooked and clipped square rug that's plastered with walnut wool, but has broken three hooks and sent me to the massage therapist twice. Yeah, yeah, I know. I'm not sitting right and my foundation is too tight. What else is new?

Like children, each rug has had its challenges and each has proven to be a gem and none are ever quite "finished." I guess I truly believe as St. Irenaeus of Lyons said that "The glory of God is a man fully alive." I know Our Heavenly Father is probably okay with my translation, "The glory of God is a hand-hooked rug naturally dyed."

Coreopsis – Suzanne's favorite yellow dye flower – grows among the vegetables in her studio garden. Georgia. 2008. *Courtesy of Suzanne Holtkamp.*

"'Frances' is a rug from my earliest naturally dyed wool. Frances Bradbury's designs lend themselves to an older, more-vintage look." From *American Hooked Rug Patterns* by Frances Bradbury. Hooked by Suzanne Holtkamp. Georgia. 2004. 22" x 27". *Courtesy of Suzanne Holtkamp.*

"The Holtkamps came to America from Hanover, Germany, in 1836. They proceeded up the Mississippi River from New Orleans and in the spring of 1837 settled in Lee County, Iowa. John and Margareth had five children. This rug commemorates their third son. Barney married Catherine (after his first wife died) and they had eleven children." "The Barney and Catherine Holtkamp Rug" was hooked on a burlap feed sack from Iowa using naturally dyed wool, linen, cotton, and velvet. "The leaves represent the children. The church remembers the first Catholic Church built in the area on Holtkamp land. And the red, white, and blue signifies the pride they felt for their new country." Designed and hooked by Suzanne Holtkamp using naturally dyed fabrics. Georgia. 2005. 28.5" x 33.5". *Courtesy of Suzanne Holtkamp.*

These are a few of the antique rugs in Suzanne's collection, which have proven to be valuable learning tools and sources of creative inspiration. "Frost #57" and one of a kind "Antique Flowers." Georgia. 2008. *Courtesy of Suzanne Holtkamp.*

"A harvest of marigolds is always a good thing." Georgia. 2008. *Courtesy of Suzanne Holtkamp.*

"The Classical Method" of dyeing as coined by Suzanne Holtkamp. Georgia. 2008. *Courtesy of Suzanne Holtkamp.*

Marigold dyed wool drying on the porch. Georgia. 2008. *Courtesy of Suzanne Holtkamp.*

"Frost #60." Edward Sands Frost, born in Maine in 1843, is often credited with being the first commercial hooked rug pattern maker. His traditional designs are still available and continue to be popular with modern day rug hookers. "I purchased this pattern from a non-hooker and since it was printed by the Henry Ford Museum I debated if I should really hook it or just leave the pattern as is. Well... the hooker duked it out (mentally) with the vintage collector, and the hooker won. I had a grand time doing it." Frost pattern on burlap printed in the late 1970s by the Henry Ford Museum, Michigan. Hooked by Suzanne Holtkamp using naturally dyed fabrics. Georgia. 2005. 27.5" x 42.5". *Courtesy of Suzanne Holtkamp.*

Gathered marigold buds soak in a stainless steel pan in preparation for the dye pot. Georgia. 2008. *Courtesy of Suzanne Holtkamp*.

Back to the 21st century and "the not so pretty method" of natural dyeing. Suzanne turns up the heat! Georgia. 2008. *Courtesy of Suzanne Holtkamp.*

The results of the modern marigold dyeing method. Georgia. 2008. *Courtesy of Suzanne Holtkamp.*

"'Roses and Scrolls' was inspired by all the research I was doing on commercial pattern maker Edward Sands Frost (1843-1894). Although not nearly as elaborate as a Frost design, I truly enjoyed the freedom of drawing this free hand without worrying about everything matching. There are several pieces of antique fabric hooked into the piece. It is long and skinny resembling a rug done during the mid-to-late 19th century, which would have been drawn on a feed sack that had been split apart." Designed and hooked by Suzanne Holtkamp using naturally dyed fabrics. Georgia. 2005. 17" x 34". *Courtesy of Suzanne Holtkamp*.

"Liberty" was inspired by a Maude Stumm (1870-1935) advertising illustration done for the Assurance Life Company. "When I saw this illustration, I was instantly mesmerized. It led me to research Maude Stumm. She primarily did water color illustrations for commercial purposes like advertising, catalogs, and calendars. This was an interesting rug to do because the wool had to show very subtle variations. I used cochineal with an iron wash. The flag was dyed with indigo." Hooked by Suzanne Holtkamp using naturally dyed fabrics. Georgia. 2006. 26.5" x 22.5". *Courtesy of Suzanne Holtkamp.*

"I bought this 'Mini Tabriz' pattern at our rug hooking chapter flea market because no one wanted a burlap pattern. (Many of today's rug hooking artists prefer to hook on more durable foundations such as linen, cotton warp or monk's cloth.) Being a dedicated recycler, I couldn't pass it up. The pattern was in like-new condition. I proceeded to use all recycled thrift store wool and dyed the colors to match an Oriental I found in a library book. I mixed all various shades of each color together to give it a worn look. The result was a hooked Oriental, which looks comfortable and aged." Designed by Jane McGown Flynn. House of Price / Charco pattern. Hooked by Suzanne Holtkamp using chemically dyed woolen fabric. Georgia. 2003. 35.5" x 48". *Courtesy of Suzanne Holtkamp.*

Using up nature dyed scraps Suzanne Holtkamp fashioned "Frost #127 – Parrot." She recalls the traditional way. "This is how you hook a rug. Take Uncle George's trousers and hook them in. When you run out, go to the scrap bag and get Aunt Rose's old skirt. Throw a few pieces into the dye pot and keep hooking. Dog fennel in bloom? Then... let's make some yellow. You get the picture." A wool blanket was used to create the rug's braided edge. Edward Sands Frost pattern. Hooked by Suzanne Holtkamp using naturally dyed woolen fabrics. Georgia. 2006. 19.5" x 36". *Courtesy of Suzanne Holtkamp.*

"This rug shows the round barn built by BJ and Cecilia Holtkamp in 1917 in Salem, Iowa. The barn was considered an architectural marvel for the area and was added to the National Historic Register in 1986. The barn still stands and remains in the family." "Holtkamp Round Barn Rug." Designed and hooked by Suzanne Holtkamp using naturally dyed woolen fabrics. Georgia. 2005. 33" x 45". *Courtesy of Suzanne Holtkamp*.

Elaine Zimney gives Margaret and Annabelle Holtkamp a proper Southern hooking lesson. Georgia. 2008. *Courtesy of Suzanne Holtkamp.*

"A good saxon blue dye day." Saxon blue, a pre-mixed solution, is used to achieve the lighter shades of true indigo. True indigo dye, the color of blue jeans, is extracted from a variety of plants most importantly the indigo plant. Nearly all indigo dye today is synthetically manufactured. Georgia. 2008. *Courtesy of Suzanne Holtkamp.*

"Cochineal reds, indigo, and saxon blue were used in making 'St. Augustine.' This rug was a challenge. I did it to demonstrate just how bright natural colors can be. The scrolls are natural dip-dyes. I had no instructions to do such a thing because dip-dyes are a relatively new idea. So I figured it out! The wool was pre-mordanted and dyed with fustic yellow. I then used either cochineal or saxon blue to get the different combinations. Rug hooking artist and teacher Eric Sandberg kindly guided me through the scroll details knowing my natural dip dyes would probably not come out exactly like chemically dyed ones." House of Price / Charco pattern. Hooked by Suzanne Holtkamp using naturally dyed fabrics. Georgia. 2003. 25.5" x 37". *Courtesy of Suzanne Holtkamp*.

"I showed up for my first official rug workshop with Eric Sandberg as my teacher with no pattern and a basket full of wool I had dyed using three Cushing colors. (W. Cushing and Company of Maine, has been making and selling Cushing 'Perfection' Dyes since 1879.) This 'Rose of Sharon' pattern was in Eric's car trunk, unclaimed because it was burlap. (Today's rug hookers prefer stronger and more durable foundations such as linen, cotton warp or monk's cloth.) I told Eric I couldn't buy any wool and this rug was born! I am a true believer in creativity that springs from limits. 'Use it up, wear it out, – Make it do or do without.' I know my grandmothers are smiling on me from up above." Heirloom Rugs pattern. Hooked by Suzanne Holtkamp using chemically dyed woolen fabrics. Georgia. 2002. 25" x 36". *Courtesy of Suzanne Holtkamp.*

"I bought this pattern at Joan Moshimer's studio in Kennebunkport while driving through on my way to Augusta, Maine, to meet with Jane Radcliffe of the Maine State Museum. I was on my way to finally meeting Jane in person after having worked together via e-mail and phone on the museum's Frost Exhibit. This rug brings back all the wonderful memories of Jane's friendship, camaraderie, and the many blessings that sprung from that exhibit. This rug will always hold a special place in my heart. The ducks live with my mother and I visit them often!" "Frost # 17 Ducks." W. Cushing and Company pattern. Hooked by Suzanne Holtkamp using naturally dyed fabrics. Georgia. 2005. 17" x 37". *Courtesy of Suzanne Holtkamp*.

"This pattern is just too fabulous to not be a bag! I used all scrap wools, naturally dyed. There are even a few felted sweater pieces mixed in." "Frost #118". Printed with permission from the Maine State Museum by Early American Rug Hooking. Hooked by Suzanne Holtkamp using naturally dyed fabrics. Georgia. 2007. 36" x 18" before sewn. *Courtesy of Suzanne Holtkamp.*

Always on the hunt for new dye sources, Suzanne Holtkamp picks dog fennel also known as stinking chamomile. This versatile plant produces a green dye. Georgia. 2008. *Courtesy of Suzanne Holtkamp.*

"'Scrap Rug' was fabulous to hook because I used leftovers and pieces of fabric like cotton that I had been experimenting with." Designed and hooked by Suzanne Holtkamp using naturally dyed fabrics. Georgia. 2004. 24" x 31". *Courtesy of Suzanne Holtkamp.*

"The famous wool cabinet. You can never have too much." Georgia. 2008. *Courtesy of Suzanne Holtkamp.*

"This rug was hooked for James and Carol Holtkamp to celebrate their 50th wedding anniversary and their life together as husband and wife. The outline of the couple in the middle was traced from their wedding photograph. The irises on either side number seven, one for each of their children. The irises are in birth order with Greg nearest the top, then Jerry, Julie (pink), Brian, Brad, Mathew, and Stanley. The couple is standing on a quilt, which shows Carol's love for creating family quilts. The background is the Iowa landscape with the Mississippi River at the far end. The house in the middle is a family homestead (now owned by Larry and Cathy Holtkamp) and the house in which James was born. The church is St. James in St. Paul, Iowa. The colors around the border are those of the Santa Fe Railroad, the company which employed Carol's father." Suzanne Holtkamp, wife of Mathew Holtkamp, using both vegetable and chemical dyes, hooked the "James and Carol Holtkamp Anniversary Rug." One piece of fabric, the center of the quilt squares, is over 170 years old to commemorate 1836, the year the first Holtkamp sailed up the Mississippi. Designed and hooked by Suzanne Holtkamp. Georgia. 2008. 36" x 60". *Courtesy of Suzanne Holtkamp.*

"'57 Chevy' was done for my father on the 50th anniversary of when he purchased this car. He still owns the car. The design was taken from an actual photograph. The sky is his old denim jeans and the ground is his awful polyester pants! It is a mixture of naturally dyed and chemically dyed wool. While completing this rug, I shared in many memories of hookers in '57 Chevys!" Designed and hooked by Suzanne Holtkamp. Georgia. 2008. 21" x 44". *Courtesy of Suzanne Holtkamp*.

Members of Atlanta's Dogwood Chapter of ATHA (Association of Traditional Hooking Artists) visit Suzanne Holtkamp's rug hooking studio. Pictured hard at work is Joan Payton, "our free spirit." Georgia. 2008. *Courtesy of Suzanne Holtkamp.*

Southern ladies all. Members of Atlanta's Dogwood Chapter of ATHA (Association of Traditional Hooking Artists) enjoy a leisurely afternoon luncheon on the porch of Suzanne Holtkamp's Buford home. Suzanne, an active member of this talented and proficient group, hosted the spring gathering. "The wearing of hats was encouraged but not required." Georgia. 2008. *Courtesy of Suzanne Holtlkamp.*

KATHIE MEYERS AND FRIENDS

Rug hooking teacher and artist Kathie Meyers, often referred to as "Mother Hen," owns a full service rug hooking shop in Fayetteville, Georgia. The "Woolen Rooster" offers everything a rug hooker could ever want; cutters, frames, hooks, patterns, woolen fabrics of every shade and texture, and more. Instruction is also available. When asked if the following rugs were the work of her students she graciously replied, "These are my friends."

Kathie Meyers

At age four, my grandmother taught me to sew doll clothes. I still have one of these crudely made treasures and the loving memories of those days of sharing. Sewing with needle and thread has been part of my life ever since, taking form in dolls, formals, home décor, and quilting. For years, I designed projects, patterns, and instructions for quilting and fabric craft books. About nine years ago, I saw my first hooked rug and took a class. Rug hooking is my true passion and I so wish I had discovered this about thirty years ago. My epitaph should say two things; "Time is the greatest luxury in life" and "Dear God, Thank you for the Sheep."

As a rug hooking artist, "'Proverbs 31:13' is very special and this pattern spoke to me the minute I saw it. Just had to hook it!" Woolen Memories pattern. Hooked by Kathie Meyers. Georgia. 2006. 23" x 36". *Courtesy of Kathie Meyers.*

This "Rustling Leaves Quilt" is displayed in Kathie Meyers's home during the fall season. Quilt pattern by Cheryl Haynes. Made by Kathie Meyers. Georgia. 2004. 56" x 40". *Courtesy of Kathie Meyers.*

"Rustling Leaves Rug," complete with patchwork background, was hooked to match the aforementioned "Rustling Leaves Quilt." Adapted from a quilt pattern by Cheryl Haynes. Hooked by Kathie Meyers. Georgia. 2005. 46" x 30". *Courtesy of Kathie Meyers.*

"I love old quilts, especially Baltimore Album appliqué styles. 'Parlor Bouquet' is my stylized version of colors and subject of these old treasures." Designed and hooked by Kathie Meyers. Georgia. 2007. 13.5" x 13.5". *Courtesy of Kathie Meyers.*

"Friendship's Garden" quilt is a decorative wall hanging displayed in Kathie Meyers's home year round. Blackbird Designs. Made by Kathie Meyers. Georgia. 2006. 49.5" x 49.5". *Courtesy of* Kathie Meyers.

"Friendship's Garden" rug was hooked to match the aforementioned wall hanging of the same name. "The pattern is actually a quilt pattern which I used and reduced in size then drew on linen. It rests under an antique table in the family room (where the quilt hangs) so that it receives very little foot traffic since the background is so light." The rug's background color was dyed to look like the muslin in the quilt. Blackbird Designs. Hooked by Kathie Meyers, Georgia. 2006. 43" x 43". *Courtesy of Kathie Meyers*.

"Came But For Friendship And Took Away Love." "To celebrate our daughter's wedding, I designed this rug as a surprise for Dana and Matt for presentation at their rehearsal dinner. My personnel challenge was to make a 'white-on-white' rug in keeping with the wedding theme and also so that colors would not distract the eye from focus on the bride. The 'whites' evolved by use of various fibers, textures, and wool from family clothing. The overall shape, flowers, and picot edge are based on her wedding gown's lace train. The bride and groom stood on the rug during the ceremony. The title, having special meaning to them, was their wedding theme." Designed and hooked by Kathie Meyers. Georgia. 2006. 25" x 29". *Courtesy of Kathie Meyers.*

The design of this special heirloom hooked rug was, in part, inspired by the lace train of Kathie Meyers's daughter's wedding gown. Georgia 2006. *Courtesy of Kathie Meyers.*

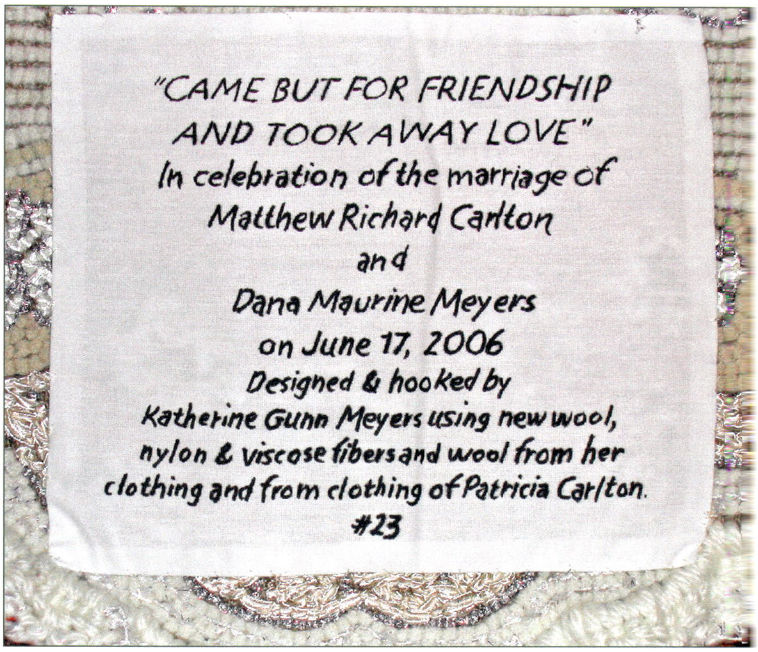

Detail of the label sewn on the back of "Came But For Friendship And Took Away Love" commemorative hooked rug. Georgia. 2006 *Courtesy of Kathie Meyers.*

"Marie," a realistic hooked study of rose buds and foliage, was made into a decorative accent pillow. Designed by Jane McGown Flynn. House of Price / Charco pattern. Hooked by Kathie Meyers. Georgia. 2008. 15" x 15". *Courtesy of Kathie Meyers.*

"Arabo," a traditional Persian-style pattern, was hooked in a very non-traditional manner using wide cut strips of woolen fabric from a limited "scrap bag" choice of colors and values. This special class, conducted by hooking artist Eric Sandberg, stretched the students' creativity and resulted in some fabulous looking rugs. Designed by Jane McGown Flynn. House of Price / Charco pattern. Hooked by Kathie Meyers. Georgia. 2007. 30" x 51". *Courtesy of Kathie Meyers.*

"A funny little rug, 'Turkey Talk' was inspired by our Southern 'Chick-Fil-A' commercials that feature standing 'Chick-Fil-A' cows holding signs declaring 'Eat Mor Chikin.'" Designed and hooked by Kathie Meyers. Georgia. 2007. 17" x 13". *Courtesy of Kathie Meyers.*

An artistically hooked still life of "Fruit" upon which to rest your head. Designed by Jane McGown Flynn. House of Price / Charco pattern. Hooked by Kathie Meyers. Georgia. 2008. 14" x 11". *Courtesy of Kathie Meyers.*

I have been involved in some type of fiber arts since early childhood, when my mother taught me to sew doll clothes, and my aunt taught me to embroider. I have tried almost every type of fiber art at this point, but my loves are quilting and rug hooking. In my real life – otherwise known as how I support these passions – I am a registered nurse. I have been nursing for thirty-nine years, with the last twelve as a nurse in a correctional setting.

"Pineapple and Flowers" was started in a class sponsored by Atlanta's Dogwood Chapter of ATHA (Association of Traditional Hooking Artists). "I was especially drawn to this pattern by the creative design of the border. It remains one of my favorite rugs." Designed Beverly Conway. Hooked by Jennie Adcock. Georgia. 2006. 21" x 30". *Courtesy of Jennie Adcock.*

"Like most artists, I think that our rugs are a true expression of where we are in our lives. This rug was started following a very stressful year and I struggled to design it – skipping from one theme to another. When I finally came up with 'Bluebird of Happiness,' it made my heart sing, and I knew that life was on an uphill swing." Inspired by a Fraktur class taught by Susan Feller of West Virginia. Designed and hooked by Jennie Adcock. Georgia. 2008. 18" x 22". *Courtesy of Jennie Adcock.*

"'Bowl of Flowers' was made in a dye/hooking class at Caraway Rug Camp, in North Carolina with teacher Kathy Meentmeyer. Each day we dyed wool using a different technique; that afternoon we had to hook the wool into our rug. This was a challenge, as we never knew what colors we would be dyeing the next day. Everyone's rugs were so different, but each was beautiful." Charco/House of Price pattern. Hooked by Jennie Adcock. Georgia. 2004. 19" x 28". *Courtesy of Jennie Adcock.*

"'Squirrel and Pumpkin' is the first rug that I hooked entirely on my own. It is far from perfect but I still love it – so did my daughter, so it lives at her house now. Someday I'll hook another one for myself." Adapted from a "Need 'L Love" pattern. Hooked by Jennie Adcock. Georgia. 2004. 13" x 26". *Courtesy of Jennie Adcock.*

"'Primitive Azeri' was completed in an Eric Sandberg class using a non-traditional primitive cut to hook this very traditional Azeri-style rug. The color scheme was limited to three colors – red, green, and brown. This approach taught me to look at color in a whole new way. What a great lesson! And fun, too!" Designed by Jane McGown Flynn. House of Price / Charco pattern. Hooked by Jennie Adcock. Georgia. 2008. 43" x 28". *Courtesy of Jennie Adcock.*

Janet Fruit

I was "discovered" in a parking lot by a hooker – Kathie Meyers. She invited me to dinner with her hooking group and that is all it took. The group is passionate about hooking and eager to teach a "newbie." My husband loves it and tells everyone I am going to spend a week at a hotel "hooking and stripping." That's alright with me… I just want to attend another rug camp.

What does a rug hooker say on her deathbed? "Just one more row before I go." Put this on my tombstone…"Just one more row."

Swimming along in a sea of wool loops, "'Mildred' was my first project. I met Kathie Meyers – a passionate rug hooker who had hooked a fish. I wanted to do one too! She is a wonderful teacher and great mentor." Adapted from an appliqué quilt pattern. Hooked by Janet Fruit. Georgia. 2007. Diameter 12". *Courtesy of Janet W. Fruit.*

A hooked pastoral vignette of two sheep resting "Under the Weeping Willow Tree." Harry M. Fraser and Co. pattern. Hooked by Janet Fruit. Georgia. 15" x 15". *Courtesy of Janet W. Fruit.*

An intricate scheme, "Celtic Knot" showcases hand-dyed woolen fabrics. Designed by Jane McGown Flynn. House of Price/Charco pattern. Hooked by Janet Fruit. Georgia. 2008 9" x 9". *Courtesy of Janet W. Fruit.*

"Twin Roses" pattern was simplified to one rose pattern, hooked with a limited palette and then made into a pillow. Gene Shepherd / Jane Olson pattern. Hooked by Janet Fruit. Georgia. 2008. 21" x 21". *Courtesy of Janet W. Fruit.*

"Tulips" was inspired by the early Pennsylvania Dutch-style of lettering and folk art known as Fraktur. West Virginia hooking artist, Susan Feller, taught this unique class. "I was delighted to design a rug myself, using the teacher's templates. Susan guided color selection and I was off and running." Designed and hooked by Janet Fruit. Georgia. 2008. 24" x 36". *Courtesy of Janet W. Fruit*.

A petite "Persian"-style design, hooked in jewel-like tones, makes for a handsome foot stool. New Earth Designs pattern. Hooked by Janet Fruit. Georgia. 2007. 12" x15". *Courtesy of Janet W. Fruit.*

Vicki Gusler

Another friend of Kathie Meyers; one who enjoys pulling those loops and hooking those rugs.

Bordered in hooked tweed, this "Tree of Life" is a simplified and stylized version of the traditional Shaker design. Ohio Farmhouse/ Star Rug Company pattern. Hooked by Vicki Gusler. Georgia. 2005. 11" x 23". *Courtesy of Vicki Gusler.*

A golden sky highlights "Crow on a Hill." Elongated lamb's tongue motifs flank the fleck-winged bird. Crow Hill Primitives pattern. Hooked by Vicki Gusler. Georgia. 2006. 14" x 25". *Courtesy of Vicki Gusler.*

A home is not a home without a Mason jar filled with "Old Buttons," hooked or otherwise. An assortment of buttons was sewn onto this hooked wall hanging. Red Saltbox pattern. Hooked by Vicki Gusler. Georgia. 2006. 21" x 12". *Courtesy of Vicki Gusler.*

"Pointed Carnation," in shades of pink, sprouts from a fanciful stem. Designed by Susan Feller / Ruckman Mill Farm pattern. Hooked by Vicki Gusler. Georgia. 2008. 17" x 13". *Courtesy of Vicki Gusler.*

Tethered pairs of oak leaves frame three fence-sitting pumpkins. – all basking in the light of a waning moon on this "Fall Night." Payton Primitives pattern. Hooked by Vicki Gusler. Georgia. 2008. 18" x24". *Courtesy of Vicki Gusler*.

Beth Riley

I first saw a hooked rug at the Georgia State Fair in 1995 and fell in love. It wasn't until six years later that I saw another one... and just in time for beginner's class. Timing is everything.

Reminiscent of Pennsylvania Dutch decorative patterns, "Tulip Cross" is vibrant against a dark background. Designed by Emma Lou Lais. Hooked by Beth Riley. Georgia. 2003. 38" x 38". *Courtesy of Beth Riley.*

"I grabbed 'Five Bunnies' before running out the door to take my husband to the ER, thinking I would be there for several hours – a great time to hook. Actually I was there for a week while he was being treated for a blockage of the intestinal kind. In memory of that event, I added something to the rug. Look closely behind the last bunny." Designed by Dianne Kelley. Hooked by Beth Riley. Georgia. 2001. 16" x 49". *Courtesy of Beth Riley.*

Simple floral motifs combine with geometric designs in this stylized "Oriental." Braid-Aid pattern. Hooked by Beth Riley. Georgia. 2002. 27" x 45". *Courtesy of Beth Riley.*

A magical mystery tour of "Towne Garden" will take you away from the stress and strife of the real world. An inward facing saw-tooth border contains the fantasy garden and home. Karen Kahle / Primitive Spirit pattern. Hooked by Beth Riley. Georgia. 2006. 31" x 41". *Courtesy of Beth Riley.*

Heavenly wings of hooked mohair sit upon the shoulders of this "Crazy Angel." She dons a sunray crown that reaches out and up toward five primitive stars echoing her pair of star-kissed checks. Designed by Carrie Martin. Hooked by Beth Riley. Georgia. 2008. 17" x 21". *Courtesy of Beth Riley*.

Laura Strawn

I, like other rug hookers, have enjoyed many different crafts and art, but rug hooking is the one thing that I love as much today as the day I first started hooking – painting with wool – how amazing!

Scrolls, fanciful or plain and found on rugs of all ages, are an important part of the rug hooking tradition. What better way to learn the techniques of hooking these ornamental designs than "Scroll Sampler." Designed by Jane McGown Flynn. House of Price / Charco pattern. Hooked by Laura Strawn. Georgia. 2008. 43" x 17". *Courtesy of Laura Strawn.*

PRIS BUTTLER
Gainesville, Georgia

My life has taken many twists and turns in the art world, from graphic designer to rug hooker to full time professional artist and rug hooking teacher. All are wonderfully interrelated and one feeds off the other. As time goes on, I cannot believe how rug hooking and painting have worked together to make a complete artist out of me. Rug hooking has introduced me to another unknown world.

Having been raised Aruba, NWI, and Caracas, Venezuela, and living most of my life in the West, I had no knowledge of this wonderful craft until I met Gainesville, Georgia's Beverly Goodrich, a much admired fiber artist in her own right.

As I moved through my painting life I found I wanted to discover more interesting things. I traveled several times to New England and Williamsburg, Virginia, and found out so many things about American folk art. Through Beverly I took an interest in rug hooking.

In compiling these rugs for this book, I found that they were all about my life and the places I had been, things I had seen and done. Each one says a little something about me and the great art that is in all mediums and cultures, past and present. And the sheer joy of color is the best thing of all.

So rather than hone in on rug hooking things such as florals and worrying about whether the rugs matched my house, I just jump in and hook what I please. As it all turns out, I discovered that all artists have a palette of colors they work in and oddly enough, all my rugs did match my house. I live in my palette, on walls and furniture.

In the beginnings of my rug hooking, I found that I wanted to tell about Southern Culture and days gone by. With the help of other rug hookers and their ideas, I began to do several about Negro culture of the South. I had spent many summers in Georgia as a child and teen and it was all stamped into my memory. I began designing rugs that have since become patterns in my catalog.

In a moment in my painting life I found I was no longer content painting folk art. I came to an impasse of what to do next. Another rug hooker friend, Pam Wiegand, also of Gainesville, Georgia, suggested that I put out a line of patterns for rug hookers. And as the old saying goes, the rest is history. One thing lead to another and Jane King gave me my first job at Caraway Rug Camp in North Carolina and bingo... I was on the teaching circuit.

And as I did Negro culture of the South, I found I had a renewed desire to paint the same thing, which I have done. And from further paintings I found new artists, such as Gustav Klimt, who is my passion of the moment for rug hooking.

As time has progressed, I have painted more, hooked more and feel that through me learning, I am a better rug hooking and painting teacher.

So it has all been a wonderful journey that I shall continue to enjoy the rest of my days.

"Railroad Worker at Lunch." Original oil painting on wood panel by Pris Buttler. "In a restaurant behind my studio (one block from the RR station) I photographed this man eating lunch." Georgia. 2003. 18" x12". *Courtesy of Pris Buttler.*

"Southern Gothic." Original oil painting on wood panel by Pris Buttler. Georgia. 2004. 16" x 20". *Courtesy of Pris Buttler*.

"At the Door." "This painting is one of many in a series displayed at the Atlanta Art Gallery." An original oil painting by Pris Buttler. Georgia. 2000. 20" x 16'. *Courtesy of Pris Butler.*

Recalling the old South. "Whole Week's Picking" was adapted from an antique watercolor of unknown artist and date. Pris Buttler Rug Designs. Designed and hooked by Pris Buttler. Georgia. 1999. 24" x 31". *Courtesy of Pris Buttler.*

"Creek Side Baptism." Original oil painting on linen canvas by Pris Buttler. Georgia. 2005. 16" x 20". *Courtesy of Jane King.*

"I wanted to hook a riverside 'Baptism' and wanted 'heavenly' sunrays (I used dip dye to accomplish this). The antique style roses were something new for me and I was unsure as to how it would all come together." Designed and hooked by Pris Butler. Georgia. 2005. 30" x 19". *Courtesy of Pris Buttler.*

A work in progress and tribute to Austrian Symbolist painter, Gustav Klimt (1862-1918.) Designed and hooked by Pris Buttler. Georgia. 2008. *Courtesy of Pris Buttler.*

"One of my favorite artists is Gustav Klimt. I took designs from a number of his paintings and designed 'VerKlempt' (translation: chocked with emotion). I found I love geometrics and don't like hooking the mirror image of one. So here I don't have to." Designed and hooked by Pris Buttler. Georgia. 2008. 34" x 48". *Courtesy of Pris Buttler*.

"I feel Vincent van Gogh is very conducive to rug hooking. The phrase around the border of the rug is from the song 'Starry, Starry Night' by Don McLean. This was a difficult rug for me because I couldn't get in van Gogh's head, which was quite disturbed." Adapted from a Vincent van Gogh painting. Hooked by Pris Buttler. Georgia. 2000. 39" x 45". *Courtesy of Pris Buttler*.

Jane Olson, the Grande Dame of California rug hooking has a sister Norma. Norma is known to wear a Minnie Pearl style hat complete with price tag. Both sisters are fun loving and talented hooking artists. "Norma saw this rug and said 'That looks just like me.' The rug had no name at the time, so I named it after her." "Norma Selene." Designed and hooked by Pris Buttler. Georgia. 2003. 29" x 19". *Courtesy of Pris Buttler.*

Detail of "Norma Selene." *Courtesy of Pris Buttler*.

GEORGIA

"Our Captain Stood Upon the Deck." "The phrase around the rug's edge came from an old whaling song. I did this rug the year after I started to hook. I had seen several whale rugs and wanted to do something different so I introduced the polar bear." Among her many talents, Pris is also known for her ability to master hooked lettering. "I learned so much about doing lettering in this rug and how to work with the weave of the backing." Pris Buttler Rug Designs. Hooked by Pris Buttler. Georgia. 1997. 40" x 46". *Courtesy of* Pris *Buttler.*

"The phrase around the edge of this rug is Latin for 'Where there is compassion and love, there is God.' I was so taken with Kim Nixon's wonderful designs after meeting her at Ramona Maddox's Castle in the Clouds Rug Camp." "Deus." Designed by Kim Nixon. Hooked by Pris Buttler. Georgia. 2002. 24" x 33". *Courtesy of Pris Buttler*.

PRIS BUTTLER RUG DESIGNS

The following rug patterns, along with many more, can be found in the *Pris Buttler Rug Designs & Ewe Two* catalog. Popular among rug hookers, the pattern designs are the original work of Pris Buttler and daughter, Christy Ancelet.

"I feel full of patriotism most of the time and have a couple of George Washington rugs in my catalog, this being one of them." Pris Buttler Rug Designs. Hooked by Pris Buttler. Georgia. 1998. 40" x 34". *Courtesy of Pris Buttler.*

"In the South sweet peas are called "English Peas," hence the name. I had visited the Victoria and Albert Museum in London and saw the beautiful tapestries and decided I wanted to design a tapestry-like rug. I wanted to vary the widths of wool I hooked with and keep the border dull so as not to compete with the inner motif. Now I have four such patterns in my catalog." Pris Buttler Rug Designs. Hooked by Pris Buttler. Georgia. 2005. 17" x 21". *Courtesy of Pris Buttler.*

"'Geometric To Dye For' was "a great exercise in using vibrant pieces of wool." Pris Buttler Rug Designs. Hooked by Pris Buttler. Georgia. 2005. 18" x 27". *Courtesy of Pris Buttler.*

“You Can’t Have My Wool Sweater.” “My first ‘real’ rug, in which I did so many things by instinct. I had no real knowledge at this point, never had a teacher, just jumped right in and did it. That’s why the grass and sky is straight line hooked. I learned so much about hooking a checker board and have never done another one!” Pris Buttler Rug Designs. Hooked by Pris Buttler. Georgia. 1996. 32″ x 52″. *Courtesy of Pris Buttler*.

Bright and snazzy, “Wool Stash” was hooked for granddaughter, Lindsey. Pris Buttler Rug Designs. Hooked by Pris Buttler. Georgia. 2008. 26″ x 30″. *Courtesy of Pris Butler.*

“Funky Chicken” was inspired by Aztec and Southwestern motifs. “I just wanted to do something fun and foolish.” Pris Buttler Rug Designs. Hooked by Pris Buttler. Georgia. 1999. 16″ x 28″. *Courtesy of Pris Buttler.*

"'Skating Angel' and 'Skating Santa,' hooked for my daughter and daughter-in-law were some of my first pieces I designed for my catalog. I felt that Christmas patterns would do well and be in demand." Pris Butler Rug Designs. Hooked by Pris Buttler. Georgia. 1999. Each 20" x 20". *Courtesy of Pris Buttler.*

"'The Quilters' is taken from one of my original folk art paintings. I worked in that art genre from 1988-1999. The wools in this rug were all dyed by me." Pris Butler Rug Designs. Hooked by Pris Buttler. Georgia. 2000. 22" x 28". *Courtesy of Pris Buttler.*

Pris Buttler admires the work of a very talented California hooking artist, author and teacher. "When I saw Gene Shepherd's finished 'Miss Weigle' rug, I became enamored of it. A friend, Donna DeYoung, bought me the pattern. I wanted to hook it very different from Gene's. It is a scrap rug, using either 'as is' or pieces of wool I have dyed. I gave this rug to Donna and she gave me a beautiful quilt." (The quilt is pictured in the following photo behind the "Sheep" pillow.) Designed by Gene Shepherd. Hooked by Pris Buttler. Georgia. 2007. 60" x 34". *Courtesy of Pris Buttler*.

"Sheep Pillow" was a "challenge" piece, assigned by hooking teacher Ingrid Hieronimus at Niagara On The Lake Rug Camp. It is embellished with ribbon and tinsel-like thread. Designed and hooked by Pris Buttler. Georgia. 2007. 15" x 25". *Courtesy of Pris Buttler.*

"Haunted Halloween" was inspired by an antique postcard. "I picked this card because of the challenges – like how to do the witch, the creepy frogs and not making the pumpkins orange." Hooked by Pris Buttler. Georgia. 2006. 26" x 17". *Courtesy of Pris Buttler.*

"I told my grandson Andrew the story of Noah's ark and asked him to draw me the ark and the animals as he saw them. The ark turned out to be a space ship (top middle) and the animals were floating in the night sky!" "Noah's Ark." Hooked by Pris Buttler. Georgia. 2002. 39" x 58". *Courtesy of Pris Buttler*.

"'Amy's Sheep,' is a spin off of 'You Can't Have My Wool Sweater.' I hooked this rug for my son and his wife for Christmas 1997. By this time I had discovered a great Atlanta hooking teacher, Mary Paul Wright. She taught me hooking and dyeing techniques." Designed and hooked by Pris Buttler. Georgia. 1997. 29" x 39". *Courtesy of Pris Buttler.*

"A wonderful friend, Bev Goodrich, taught me to hook. I went to a local fabric store and got wool blends and hooked right off the bolt. Choices were extremely limited so Bev gave me a piece of gold wool. The rest is history. 'Pris and John's Zodiac Rug' was inspired by my husband's and my Chinese Zodiac signs. This is my first rug." Designed and hooked by Pris Buttler. Georgia. 1996. 18" x 23". *Courtesy of Pris Buttler.*

The story behind "Pris' Folk Art Rug."

I was quite taken by the folk life rugs I was seeing in shows and decided I should do one. As a designer I felt the borders that are designed after the Azeri rugs with Oriental feel were not in keeping with American story rugs.

Consequently, having been born in Texas, I thought I'd like a Texas border, since it was a major part of my life. The Long Horn cattle are fading out of the lower border. I got this idea from the Navajo rug makers of the Southwest. They always weave one thread (an imperfection) to the outside of the rug, to let the spirits in and out.

On the top left is the Island of Aruba where I grew up and lived until I was twelve. My father worked for Esso, hence the refinery. My mother surf fished. I was born in 1943 and the German U-boats used to torpedo oil tankers outside the harbor during World War II.

The three trees are peach trees for my childhood summers in Georgia and where I now reside. The Scottie dogs were all our dogs and Jaquito, our one cat. The black and white cats are the ones from my childhood. Pictured are my brothers Mark (the sailor) and Toby (a heart transplant survivor). I am swimming in the ocean in Aruba. The city under the submarine is Caracas, Venezuela where I spent my teen years.

My husband and I married in New Mexico. The goat is for our zodiac sign – "Capricorn" – we are both born on the same day.

The palette is for my present life. Pictured is my son skiing Colorado where we lived and my daughter being chased by a goose that tormented her at my mother's house. She also was in 4H and did cake decorating in Colorado.

Bottom left is me with my six grandchildren, daughter-in-law and son-in-law.

Pine trees are at the cemetery where I will be buried, "Sunrise Cemetery," and the rugs are for hooking in heaven.

"Pris' Folk Art Rug." Designed and hooked by Pris Buttler. Georgia. 2002. 56" x 40". *Courtesy of Pris Buttler.*

Reflecting on what lies ahead, accomplished painter and hooking artist, Pris Buttler holds her hooked doll "grandkids," Phillip, Lindsey and Chad. Designed and hooked by Pris Buttler. Georgia. 2008. 27" tall. *Courtesy of Pris Buttler.*

THE CRESCENT LANE RUG HOOKERS
AKA The Heavenly Hookers

Almost every Monday, the Crescent Lane Rug Hookers, also known as the Heavenly Hookers gather at Nancy Thompson's Heavenly Hook Nook, a circa 1800 cabin where "laughter, camaraderie, and hooking fills the Athens, Georgia, air." Pictured here and also throughout this book is hooked work of these talented and prolific artists.

In the words of Ansley Wiegand Crisler, "My mom hooked with my grandmother for years. When my grandmother passed, mom put her hook down because it made her so sad. Mom and I quilted for a while, and one day at the quilt shop, Mom got Nancy Thompson's and the Heavenly Hooker's book, *Hooking on the Hill*. Nancy's poem says, "I just snip out my sorrow and hook in my joy.' And really, the whole book was and is an inspiration. Mom called the next day to tell me she'd be coming to Athens – she was joining the Crescent Lane Rug Hookers... And I said, 'Well then... so am I!' And we've shared so many wonderful experiences since."

Nancy Thompson

A true Southern lady, hooking artist Nancy Thompson works on her latest project. Georgia. 2009. *Courtesy of Nancy Butts Thompson*

Originally designed as a pillow top, the "Rose of Sharon" motif was, at Nancy Thompson's request, enlarged into a handsome rug pattern. Diagonal bands, playing light against dark, form a dramatic background for stylized flowers that are reminiscent of Victorian carpeting. Designed by Jeanne Benjamin / New Earth Designs. Hooked by Nancy Thompson. Georgia. 2007. 50.5" x 50.5" *Courtesy of Nancy Butts Thompson*.

Hanging from the rough-hewn walls of the circa 1800 "Heavenly Hook Nook" cabin is "Pineapples, Pomegranates, and Padulas," a mirror image design of stylized fruit and fanciful flowers. "This rug speaks to me." Designed by Monika Jones / Folk Art Landing. Hooked by Nancy Thompson. Georgia. 2008. 79" x 38". *Courtesy of Nancy Butts Thompson.*

Lollipop flowers, numbering a lucky seven, spring forth from a decorative container. A pair of stars and lamb's tongue border completed the folk art still life. "Flowers and Stars." Designed by Kris Miller / Spruce Ridge Studios. Hooked by Nancy Thompson. Georgia. 2006. 26" x 35". *Courtesy of Nancy Butts Thompson.*

A plaid hooked vessel grounds curlicue stems of crewel inspired buds and blossoms. A bold red and blue central tulip motif dominates the arrangement. Inspiration for "Ipswich" came from an early New England craved chair back. Edyth O'Neill Design. Woolley Fox. Hooked by Nancy Thompson. Georgia. 2005. 27" x 34". *Courtesy of Nancy Butts Thompson.*

Motivated by Susan Feller's Fraktur class, Nancy Thompson used templates and old images to design her own Pennsylvania German folk art. An angel on high surveys all. "Fraktur Wall Hanging." Hooked by Nancy Thompson. Georgia. 2006. 33" x 22". *Courtesy of Nancy Butts Thompson.*

"DonnaSue Shaw, the designer of 'Fountain of Eweth' lives on an island in Vermont and her world and mine are very different. I'm much older – say 'y'all' a lot, and have to wrap up in a blanket at 60 degrees – and yet, sight unseen, we have become friends. I love her designs and would hook them all if time permitted. I'm addicted to rug hooking! That sums it up!" Designed by DonnaSue Shaw / Primitive Grace. Hooked by Nancy Thompson. Georgia. 2007. 37" x 24.5". *Courtesy of Nancy Butts Thompson*.

A light background highlights another of Nancy Thompson's Fraktur wall hangings. Note the male and female birds at the crest of the display. Designed and hooked by Nancy Thompson. Georgia. 2005. 25" x 20". *Courtesy of Nancy Butts Thompson.*

Quilting designs and embroidery motifs converge. Floral vines, complete with berries and birds, are positioned around ten bow tie hit or miss stripe squares. Designed by Monika Jones. / Folk Art Landing. Hooked by Nancy Thompson. Georgia. 2007. 35" x 53". *Courtesy of Nancy Butts Thompson.*

"I asked my friend and rug hooking teacher, Eric Sandberg to design a rug for my expected granddaughter. Happily enough, the rug was hanging in her room when she was born in January of 2008." "Morgan Murray's Paper Doll Rug." Hooked by Nancy Thompson. Georgia. 2007. 25" x36". *Courtesy of Nancy Butts Thompson*.

"'Tom and Huck' was inspired by the fabric in my grandson's room and is hanging over the fireplace in the room of Jack Murray Jr." Hooked by Nancy Thompson. Georgia. 2007. 30" x 36". *Courtesy of Nancy Butts Thompson*.

"Horse Feather" is a simple little rug complete with equine folk art. Folk Art Rugs. Hooked by Nancy Thompson. Georgia. 2006. 22" x 40". *Courtesy of Nancy Butts Thompson.*

"'Skunk's Welcome' was designed to commemorate "when the husband of designer DonnaSue Shaw flushed nineteen skunks from under their home in Vermont. This rug was created as a way to tease Michael, I think, as he probably has a resentment toward spraying skunks." Designed by DonnaSue Shaw / Primitive Grace. Hooked by Nancy Thompson. Georgia. 2008. 19" x32". *Courtesy of Nancy Butts Thompson.*

LaFreda Baird

LaFreda Baird, one of the first members of Nancy Thompson's Heavenly Hookers, fashioned "Georgia Bulldog" to honor the UGA's favorite mascot. Designed by Nancy Thompson using templates. Hooked by LaFreda Baird. Georgia. 2008. 14" x14". *Courtesy of La Freda Baird.*

Paula Barlett

Recalling vintage appliqué bed coverings, a pair of "Quilted Cats" frolic among berries and bird. The outer vine border includes running bunnies. A charming folk art piece. Designed by Pat Cross. Hooked by Paula Bartlett. Georgia. 2007. 29" x 33". *Courtesy of Paula Bartlett.*

"Shah Abbas," is a Persian-style hooked rug of intricate design. The green inner field was horizontally hooked to mimic hand-woven and knotted carpets. A fringe was added to complement the work. Designed by Jane McGown Flynn. House of Price / Charco. Hooked by Paula Barlett. Georgia. 2008. 78" x 40". *Courtesy of Paula Bartlett.*

Cynthia Bell

"My sister, Beverly Winsness started 'Shaker Tree' twenty years ago before I even knew what rug hooking was. She had all of the design hooked and some of the background. She moved away from her rug hooking friends and never finished it. When I began rug hooking, a few years back, she gave it to me to do whatever I wanted with it. After years in my closet, I pulled it out and finished it for her birthday!" Lib Callaway Patterns. Hooked by Cynthia Bell. Georgia. 2008. 28" x 37". *Courtesy of Cynthia Bell.*

"My friend, Nancy Thompson gave me this pattern as a gift because I fell in love with hers. 'Garden Path' is the sweetest little rug and so much fun to hook." It was created from "mostly gizzards from my gizzard box." (Translation: leftovers from the scrap box.) Karen Kahle / Primitive Spirit pattern. Hooked by Cynthia Bell. Georgia. 2008. 30" x 17". *Courtesy of Cynthia Bell.*

A garden delight for one's derriere; "Big Sunflower" seat cushion. Sunny buns are happy buns! Designed and hooked by Cynthia Bell. Georgia. 2008. 18" x 17". *Courtesy of Cynthia Bell.*

Overlapping clamshells contain a bouncing bunny. "The Bunny Rug." Designed and hooked by Cynthia Bell. Georgia. 2006. 22.5" x 28". *Courtesy of Cynthia Bell.*

Bands and stripes of both tweed and solid colored wools frame this charming hooked portrait of a little furry friend. "'LuLu' is an older dog belonging to my daughter's in-laws. I wanted to give them a rug of her so they will always have her around." Designed and hooked by Cynthia Bell. Georgia. 2008. 19.5" x 25". *Courtesy of Cynthia Bell.*

Nancy Blackburn

"My sister tatted a beautiful table cloth for me so I decided to hook six chair seat covers for her. She had just refinished a dining room set and I thought this color combination would bring out the grain in the wood and enhance the antiquity of the set." "Letter 'D' with Vine." Designed and hooked by Nancy Blackburn. Georgia. 2008. 21" x 18". *Courtesy of Nancy Blackburn*.

Margo Candelario

"I hooked 'Original Genesis' for a visual art exhibition at the University of Connecticut entitled 'The 3rd Eye – A Study of Transition from the Perspective of A Widow.' Because I am a visual artist, hooking has allowed me to explore another art form using my own designs." Designed and hooked by Margo Candelario. Georgia. 2008. 41" x 31". *Courtesy of Margo Candelario.*

Pat Cardin

"Funky Chicken" struts his stuff and brightens Pat Cardin's kitchen. Pris Buttler Rug Designs. Hooked by Pat Cardin. Georgia. 2008. 18" x 28". *Courtesy of Pat Cardin.*

Joyce Carey

"I'm a retired antique dealer and started hooking in 2001 after seeing rugs of a fellow dealer. I enjoy hooking patterns by others as well as designing my own. 'Gabbea,' a story telling rug, was started in a class taught by Eric Sandberg. I made the rug 'mine' by choosing colors that are not realistic. I enjoyed hooking the water with a rose and green plaid and adding red fish. My camel driver and water carrier are dark skinned. The camels were hooked from a variety of brown plaids." Designed by Jane McGown Flynn. House of Price / Charco. Hooked by Joyce Carey. Georgia. 2008. 54" x 34". *Courtesy of Joyce Carey.*

Mimicking women's handwork of an earlier time, rug hookers replicate centuries old yarn sewn bed "ruggs." This colorful "Bed Rugg," meant for floor use, was adapted from a drawing in *Needlework in America* by Virginia Churchill. Hooked by Joyce Carey. Georgia. 2006. 60" x 51". *Courtesy of Joyce Carey.*

"Love Flute" was adapted, with permission, from an original illustration found in artist and author Paul Goble's book, *Love Flute*. "My mother lives in Tucson, Arizona, and this rug was hooked especially for her." In addition to working with strips of woolen fabric, Joyce Carey added a suede and leather braid to the head of the male figure and glass beads into the braid of the flute player. Adapted into a rug hooking pattern by Lisa C. Van Meter. Hooked by Joyce Carey. Georgia. 2003. 31" x 42". *Courtesy of Joyce Carey.*

Judy Carter

"Fountain of Eweth," combines Judy Carter's love of sheep and hooking. "My mother had suffered with Alzheimer's disease for years and I was her primary care giver. While sitting in my doctor's office, weeping through my yearly physical, she looked at me and said, 'You will get a hobby!' The rest is history…and I thank God for the blessing me with a wonderful rug hooking guild." Judy Carter is a member of the Crescent Lane Rug Hooking Guild – another Heavenly Hooker. Designed by DonnaSue Shaw / Primitive Grace. Hooked by Judy Carter. Georgia. 2008. 38" x 25". *Courtesy of Judy Carter.*

"It took me a year, but it looks great in my foyer!" This cheerful rug of mille-fleur-like design adds a note of cheer to any home. "201A Stella Hay" was named for a popular East Coast rug hooking artist, teacher, and author. Lib Callaway Designs. Hooked by Judy Carter. Georgia. 2006. 42" x 70". *Courtesy of Judy Carter.*

Joyce Connell

"In 2003 my good friend Gail Bishop invited me to Nancy Thompson's to see some hooking artists at work. I've been hooking ever since. My style of hooking is more whimsy and folky." "Don't Fry Your Favorite Chicken" features a portrait of Mammy, the iconic Southern earth mother. "I love fried chicken, but I wouldn't think of eating one that had a pet name." Designed and hooked by Joyce Connell. Georgia. 2006. 60" x 25". *Courtesy of Joyce Connell.*

Ansley Wiegand Crisler

"I was just stopping by Nancy Thompson's Heavenly Hook Nook and was in between rugs. Nancy had a large selection of smaller patterns. I chose 'Fraktur Flower' and decided to start it right away. The center of the flower was hooked that night with Nancy's scraps. Sometimes no plan is the best plan!" The finished hooked flower pattern was then made into an accent pillow, complete with cording and fringe. Designed by Susan Feller / Ruckman Mill Farm. Hooked by Ansley Wiegand Crisler. Georgia. 2007. 13" x 12". *Courtesy of Ansley Wiegand Crisler.*

"Creatures In the Night" was created at a Fraktur workshop conducted by Susan Feller. "My husband and I met at Georgia Southern University – where the Eagles soar! When I decided to hook this eagle, I wanted to add the more delicate creatures of the dark. I have always loved the sounds of the South at night." Designed by Ansley Wiegand Crisler using Fraktur tracings, templates, and original drawings. Hooked by Ansley Wiegand Crisler. Georgia. 2008. 21" x 33". *Courtesy of Ansley Wiegand Crisler.*

Madelon Dickerson

"I love the undersea world and had been on vacation in the Caribbean when I was inspired to create 'My Next Life.' This is my third hooked piece and I got carried away with the design. I had wanted to do a thin runner. When I brought my design to the Heavenly Hookers on Monday afternoon, they were horrified at the size and my lack of experience. I finished this rug in eight months, with the attitude, 'I'll show you!'" Designed and hooked by Madelon Dickerson. Georgia. 2008. 4' x 6'. *Courtesy of Madelon Dickerson.*

Shirley Dillard

"I started hooking in 2000 because my friend, Nancy Thompson had gone to Ramona Maddox's Castle in the Clouds Rug School. She was so excited about hooking she encouraged me to try. I have loved it ever since." "Bradley Primitive" offers reverse images of petite cornucopia-like scrolls overflowing with fanciful flowers, foliage, and pussy willow stalks. Leaves frame contain the floral arrangements. Harry M. Fraser Co. pattern. Hooked by Shirley Dillard. Georgia. 2006. 38" x 52". *Courtesy of Shirley Dillard.*

"Hooking is the best hobby I've ever had." "Beacon Antique" recalls folk art rugs of the late 1800s. Even distribution of color makes for an aesthetically pleasing rug. New Earth Designs. Hooked by Shirley Dillard. Georgia. 2007. 32" x 48". *Courtesy of Shirley M. Dillard.*

Piercing eyes follow all who view this hooked portrait of "Wolf." Hooked for grandson, Justin Byrd; "He loves the outdoor world and said a wolf rug would be nice." Adapted with permission from a calendar photograph. Hooked by Shirley Dillard. Georgia. 2007. 18.5" x 25.5". *Courtesy of Shirley M. Dillard*.

"Proddy Sheep" combines hooking with prodding, an old technique of poking short pieces of fabric through a woven base. A hand-dyed and hooked sky highlights the curly topped sheep, three-dimensional flowers and a nearby dragonfly that watches the world through pearl eyes. Designed by Gail Dufresne / Goat Hill Designs. Hooked by Shirley Dillard. 2008. 22" x 20". *Courtesy of Shirley M. Dillard.*

A decorative center of Pennsylvania Dutch influence is framed by a cheerful edging of over lapping lamb's tongue design. Designed by Susan Feller / Ruckman Mill Farm. Free pattern in *Colonial Reproductions and Design.* Fall 2005. Hooked by Shirley Dillard. Georgia. 2008. 53" x 18". *Courtesy of Shirley M. Dillard.*

A study in blue; "Small Basket." Designed by Susan Feller / Ruckman Mill Farm. Hooked by Shirley Dillard. Georgia. 2008. 12" x16". *Courtesy of Shirley M. Dillard.*

Carolyn Folsom

The inspiration for "Mischievous" came from a Brandon Mably design in Kaffe Fassett's book, *Welcome Home.* The wide-eyed cat in jailhouse-striped fur looks to find more mischief in his bubble-filled world. Hooked by Carolyn Folsom. Georgia. 2003. 34" x 42". *Courtesy of Carolyn Folsom.*

Originally used to decorate barns, hex signs compose a lively "PA Dutch." Designed and hooked by Carolyn Folsom. Georgia. 2007. 28" x 28". *Courtesy of Carolyn Folsom.*

Borrowing a swatch of vintage "Calico" to make a cheerful hooked rug. New Earth Designs. Hooked by Carolyn Folsom. Georgia. 2006. 24" x 36". *Courtesy of Carolyn Folsom.*

This hooked siren of the sea is embellished with beads and shells and metallic threads and yarns. Sailors beware! "Mermaid." Pris Buttler Rug Designs. Hooked by Carolyn Folsom. Georgia. 2007. 28" x 20". *Courtesy of Carolyn Folsom.*

A spirited night was had by all! Hooking artist Carolyn Folsom utilized a palette of many colors then surrounded the spooky scene with a dentil molding fence constructed with Jack O' Lantern's missing teeth. Designed by Eric Sandberg. Hooked by Carolyn Folsom. Georgia. 2008. 36" x 34". *Courtesy of Carolyn Folsom.*

Five miniature flowers sprout up from a striped goblet-like urn. Stalks of button flowers stand guard. The significance of the 1877 date is unknown. "Amherst Floral." Black Sheep Wool Designs. Hooked by Carolyn Folsom. Georgia. 2008. 41" x 29". *Courtesy of Carolyn Folsom.*

A vintage patriotic image is updated. Pictured from left to right in "Vote 2008" are candidates Obama, Clinton, Huckabee, and McCain. Adapted from "America the Beautiful." Designed by Susan Feller / Ruckman Mill Farm. Hooked by Carolyn Folsom. Georgia. 2008. 30" x 48". *Courtesy of Carolyn Folsom*.

"'Soaring' was created as a celebration rug for my son Tom's new book, *The Mad Ones*. From a cabin in Pennsylvania to writing books in New York City; the eagle is symbolic of Tom." Tom Folsom's *The Mad Ones* chronicles the rise and fall of the infamous Gallo brothers and their involvement with New York City's Underworld. Symbolism abounds in this commemorative rug. The country quilt patch border gives way to structures of concrete and steel as a darkening night sky envelops the city. Designed by Eric Sandberg. Hooked by Carolyn Folsom. Georgia. 2008. 37" x 29". *Courtesy of Carolyn Folsom.*

Patricia French

Home Sweet Home. "My husband asked me to hook a picture of our home." "French House," complete with beloved pets and significant dates is a hooked heirloom to be treasured. Designed by Eric Sandberg. Hooked by Patricia French. Georgia. 2008. 23.5" x 35". *Courtesy of Patricia French.*

An ornate central medallion dominates Persian-style "Second Thought." Jewel and earth tones play against a background of rich reds. House of Price / Charco pattern. Hooked by Patricia French. Georgia. 2007. 36" x 21". *Courtesy of Patricia French.*

Louise Chamblee Guy

Louise Chamblee Guy is a dedicated rug hooker who has always been interested in Bible stories. After open-heart surgery she was unable to complete Noah's Ark. With the help of hooking artist and teacher Candace Ballard the project was completed. "I will always love her for accepting the job." Port Primitives. Hooked by Louise Chamblee Guy and Candace Ballard. Georgia. 2007. 38" x 42". *Courtesy of Louise Chamblee Guy.*

"I love old friends, old manners, old collectibles – sugar chests, tool chests, oil lamps, gas lamps, and old rugs. And I have always loved roosters and barnyard friends." Grapes and rows of stone frame nonchalant fowl. "Vineyard Chickens." Port Primitives. Hooked by Louise Chamblee Guy. Georgia. 1999. 26" x 36". *Courtesy of Louise Camblee Guy.*

Jane Hague

As Jane Hague's New York painting friends took up hooking, she resisted. Only after they visited her in Georgia was she persuaded to visit Nancy Thompson's Crescent Lane Rug Hooking Guild. From that point on she was hooked. Recalling Pennsylvania Dutch folk art, the oddly named "Country Christmas," complete with imaginary flowers and birds by the pair, speaks of simpler times. Free pattern by Ruth Snyder – *Rug Hooking* magazine. Hooked by Jane Hague. Georgia. 2006. 33" x 26". Courtesy of Jane Hague.

Georgia Kimball

A diamondback snake with piercing eyes closes in on "Adam and Eve." The fall from Paradise awaits the au natural pair. Tomorrow's Heirlooms. Hooked by Georgia Kimball. Georgia. 2005. 24" x 38". *Courtesy of Georgia Kimball.*

This "Flowerbox" contains a whimsical and wobbly village and out of this world blossoming trees. Hooked in rich earthy tones. Karen Kahle / Primitive Spirit pattern. Hooked by Georgia Kimball. Georgia. 2006. 25" x 37". *Courtesy of Georgia Kimball.*

Sheep, flax plants, and a rug hooker at work join a Biblical saying near and dear to many hooking artists. Woolen Memories. Hooked by Georgia Kimball. Georgia. 2008. 22" x 36". *Courtesy of Georgia Kimball.*

Bonnie Lovejoy

"I live in a sparsely inhabited area in the north Georgia mountains. A few of us get together each week to hook. A metal bear plaque that hangs at my neighbor and hooking teacher's front door inspired "Bears of Sassafras Mountain," my second piece of rug hooking. I made it to cover a blanket chest my husband built." A hooked painted sky enhances the rugged landscape. Designed and hooked by Bonnie Lovejoy. Georgia. 2008. 16" x 43". *Courtesy of Bonnie Jandrew Lovejoy.*

Liz Lohse

While studying to be a Home Economics teacher Liz Lohse did a lot of tailoring. "Hooking with four decades of wool scraps from numerous projects was fun and interesting. The quiet chatter and raucous laughter of the Crescent Lane Rug Hookers filled many Monday afternoons. All those years of working with plaids and woven woolen has paid off in learning rug hooking." "Hoot to Toot." Designed and hooked by Liz Lohse. Georgia. 2008. 11" x 14". *Courtesy of Liz Lohse*.

Bobbie Monk

Curlicue scrolls dance around a medallion of "Bright Flowers." The veins of the scrolls reflect the colors used to hook the center motif. Pattern maker unknown. Hooked by Bobbie Monk. Georgia. 2008. 23" x 38". *Courtesy of Bobbie H. Monk..*

Noreen Morrison

Rug hookers persevere. "I fell in June of 2003 and broke all the fingers on my right hand. I could not hook for almost a year and a half. I have adapted to my situation after three surgeries and I am now hooking everyday." This "Bowl of Flowers" was hooked as a house-warming gift for Noreen Morrison's daughter. Bright trumpet-like blossoms mingle with folk art ferns. Designed by Ramona Orihill. Hooked by Noreen Morrison. Georgia. 2006. 18" x 27". *Courtesy of Noreen Morrison.*

A simple little "Nosegay" was Noreen Morrison's first hooking project. "I borrowed a hook and used a simple wooden hoop. This rug was done to see if I wished to pursue this hobby. Of course, I was 'hooked.'" Designed by Eric Sandberg. Hooked by Noreen Morrison. Georgia. 2002. 19.5" x 19". *Courtesy of Noreen Morrison.*

Lynne Moseman

"We added a sun porch to our home and needed some pillows to 'jazz' it up." Lynne Moseman picked up her hook and went to work creating a trio of delightful hooked and fringed accent pieces. From left to right "Bennington Basket," "Fraktur Rose," and "Bird's Lunch." All three designed by Susan Feller / Ruckman Mill Farm. Hooked by Lynne Moseman. Georgia. 2008. Each 9" x 12". *Courtesy of Lynne Moseman.*

A bit of comfort for the eye and back after a long day of working on the farm. "I hooked this 'Rooster' for Becky Stevens, my friend of 37 years. The Stevens live on a farm in Maxeys, Georgia and have an interesting array of animals; goats, chickens, pea hens, dogs, cats, and a donkey and peacock." Designed by Joyce Connell. Hooked by Lynne Moseman. Georgia. 2006. 12" x 9". *Courtesy of Lynne Moseman.*

"After my dear friend, Becky Stevens lost her beloved pet dog I asked her daughter, Kelly Stevens Anderson, a local artist, to draw a likeness of 'Boomer' on linen so I could hook a Christmas gift for Becky. Kelly also supplied me with photographs so I could get his markings right. It was quite a challenge to hook a black and white dog but we are all happy with the results and all still miss Boomer." Designed by Kelly Stevens Anderson. Hooked by Lynne Moseman. Georgia. 2007. 9" x 12". *Courtesy of Lynne Moseman.*

Clarice Scott

Exploring the world "From a Butterfly's View" gives us a close up look at an imaginary world. Designed by Susan Feller / Ruckman Mill Farm. Hooked by Clarice Scott. Georgia. 2007. 26" x 36". *Courtesy of Clarice Scott.*

CONNIE FLETCHER
Marietta, Georgia

Connie Fletcher started hooking in 1990. Her hooked pieces of art, often given as gifts, are reflections of her life and the lives of those so honored to receive her work.

Although arthritis has slowed Connie's ability to hook rugs, she continues to paint in oils and acrylics and teaches at a local senior center.

"My grandson asked me to hook a rug for him. At the time he was little and asked for a car, a train, a plane, and a boat. I wanted the rug to carry into adulthood. He told me after I gave it to him that he looked at it every night before going to sleep. As a student at Georgia Tech, 'Locomotion' was still over his bed." Designed and hooked by Connie Fletcher. Georgia. 1996. 36" x 48". *Courtesy of Connie Fletcher.*

"'Appalachian Sunset' is a memorial piece to my son who hiked 400 miles of the Appalachian Trail. It now hangs over my desk in my studio." Designed and hooked by Connie Fletcher. Georgia. 1997. 26" x 36". *Courtesy of Connie Fletcher.*

"Pink Magnolia" pillow. "My daughter lives in Pennsylvania and wanted me to hook something that reminded her of Georgia." Designed and hooked by Connie Fletcher. Georgia. 1998. 14" x 14". *Courtesy of Connie Fletcher*.

"This was designed for a friend who is a patron of the dance. I tried to convey movement in the piece." "Dancers" received Best in Show in 2000 at the Decorah, Iowa, Rug Show. Designed and hooked by Connie Fletcher. 1999. 31" x 38". *Courtesy of Connie Fletcher*.

"This hanging depicts all the places my daughter has lived. The center represents Monterey, California, where she was born. She has three sons and now lives in Pennsylvania. She wanted it in the craftsman style and was influenced by Frank Lloyd Wright." Designed and hooked by Connie Fletcher. Georgia. 1999. 4' x 5'. *Courtesy of Connie Fletcher.*

"My friend has two daughters who attended the University of Arizona and had made many trips out West. Also years ago I visited Arizona and remember how beautiful it is and so I was inspired to do 'Red Rock Canyon.'" Designed and hooked by Connie Fletcher. Georgia. 2001. 38" x 31". *Courtesy of Connie Fletcher.*

"A special friend earned a PhD in psychology in her middle years. I was so impressed and proud that I did this hooked hanging for her. The rectangles represent her calling and the many levels of the psyche. The symbols, etc., all have personal meaning." "Constance." Designed and hooked by Connie Fletcher. Georgia. 2001. 38" x31". *Courtesy of Connie Fletcher*.

"Barn Owl at Night" was designed and hooked at the request of the Vesterheim Museum in Decorah, Iowa for their fund raising auction. Designed and hooked by Connie Fletcher. Georgia. 2002. 20" x 30". *Courtesy of Connie Fletcher.*

BEVERLY GOODRICH
Gainesville, Georgia

Beverly Goodrich grew up on a dairy farm in upstate New York. After making a few stops along the way, she took her artistic talents and headed south. Married to her high school sweetheart, the mother of three daughters, and grandmother to five, Beverly has always been interested in the arts. Wood carving, jewelry making, and folk art painting are just a few of her many accomplishments. But a hooking class at Sandy Gilliam's Folk Art Shop in Roswell convinced the Georgia transplant that she should also be hooking rugs. The following, all of original design, represents a diverse sampling of Beverly Goodrich's hooking skills.

Beverly Goodrich's impressionistic "Self Portrait" was hooked in a group setting under the direction of rug hooking master, Diane Phillips. Drawn by Rae Harrell. Hooked by Beverly Goodrich. Georgia. 2005. 17.5" x 15.5". *Courtesy of Beverly A. Goodrich.*

A crowd of "Faces" comes in handy for carrying rug hooking supplies. Designed and hooked by Beverly Goodrich. Georgia. 2008. 21.5" x 15". *Courtesy of Beverly A. Goodrich.*

Waste not, want not. This hooked "Face Make-Do" is a take off on antique make-do pin cushions that were fashioned out of broken candle stick holders. Designed and hooked by Beverly Goodrich. Georgia. 2007. 14" high. *Courtesy of Beverly A. Goodrich.*

Under the direction of artist Kim Nixon, also known as "The Queen of Hooked Foot Stools," Beverly Goodrich's own "Face Stool" came to life. What a treat to rest your weary tootsies on someone's hooked head! Designed and hooked by Beverly Goodrich. Georgia. 2005. 11.5" x 15". *Courtesy of Beverly A. Goodrich.*

"Flowers in a Basket" was hooked with leftover scraps or "gizzards" as they are called in The Deep South. A lamb's tongue border with concentric circle corners frames the lively hooked mat. Designed and hooked by Beverly Goodrich. Georgia. 2008. 19" x 19.5". *Courtesy of Beverly A. Goodrich.*

Hooking artists are often inspired by quilt patterns as was Beverly Goodrich when she created "Log Cabin. Her vibrant interpretation of an old popular pattern would complement an antique or modern décor or any décor in between. Designed and hooked by Beverly Goodrich. Georgia. 2000. 29" x 53". *Courtesy of Beverly A. Goodrich.*

Part New Englander at heart, Georgia's Beverly Goodrich has a love for "Nantucket Island." She often visits the historic whaling community to spend time with special friends and that "keeps bringing me back to doing island rugs." Under full sail, an American schooner heads out to sea on a calm autumn day. Designed and hooked by Beverly Goodrich. Georgia. 1996. 34" x 49". *Courtesy of Beverly A. Goodrich.*

The navigational tool of sea faring men and women, this "Mariner's Compass" rests on a calm and reflective hooked sea. Adapted from an antique rug. Hooked by Beverly Goodrich. Georgia. 2004. 31" x 39.5". *Courtesy of Beverly A. Goodrich.*

Once considered the whaling capital of the world, Beverly Goodrich's visits to the historic Massachusetts island inspired her to hook "Nantucket Whaling." Roping frames the turbulent struggle between man and the largest of all sea mammals. Designed and hooked by Beverly Goodrich. 1997. 24" x 40". *Courtesy of Beverly A. Goodrich*.

A "Fisherman at the Helm" tightly grasps the wheel as tweed storm clouds gather and white caps form. Beverly Goodrich tips her hook to those who go down to the sea in ships. Note the initials and date hooked into the wheelbase. Designed and hooked by Beverly Goodrich. Georgia. 2002. 29" x 24". *Courtesy of Beverly A. Goodrich.*

A collage of all things "Nantucket Island" fill both the land and sea. Designed and hooked by Beverly Goodrich. Georgia. 2005. 34" x 49". *Courtesy of Beverly A. Goodrich.*

Primitive and naïve, Beverly Goodrich's talent as a folk art painter is evident in "Adam and Eve," her first hooked rug. "I was so excited about hooking I finished it in four weeks." Designed and hooked by Beverly Goodrich. Georgia. 1992. 22.5" x 35". *Courtesy of Beverly A. Goodrich.*

Beverly Goodrich's "Adam and Eve Purse" makes it fashionable to tote the first couple. You will think you are in Paradise! Birds appear and angels look down on the Garden of Eden. The flip side reveals a menagerie of Biblical animals. Designed and hooked by Beverly Goodrich. Georgia. 2008. 14" x 11". *Courtesy of Beverly A. Goodrich.*

Her "Angels" are all stars to a loving grandmother. "This represents my five wonderful grandchildren." Angelic flying figures soar among the primitive stars in a folk art tribute and cherished family heirloom. Designed and hooked by Beverly Goodrich. Georgia. 2007. 31" x 36". *Courtesy of Beverly A. Goodrich.*

Back to where it all began. "Memories on the Farm." "I started with a large piece of burlap and kept adding to the design as memories flooded in." An adopted daughter of The Deep South, Beverly Goodrich recalls her childhood home in upstate New York." Designed and hooked by Beverly Goodrich. Georgia. 1996. 29" x 52". *Courtesy of Beverly A. Goodrich.*

The blowing of horns on "Gabriel's Sun" signals good things to come. In addition to hooking with cut strips of woolen fabric, Beverly Goodrich has given the sun and angels hooked yarn hairdos. Inspired by a Fraktur. Designed and hooked by Beverly Goodrich. Georgia. 1992. 11.5" x 35.5". *Courtesy of Beverly A. Goodrich.*

MARTHA MORRIS – HOOKING A HUNDRED RUGS

Martha Morris, a native of Tampa, Florida, hooked her first rug in 1968 while living in New Canaan, Connecticut. On a trip to the Fraser Rug Studio, located outside of Hartford, she purchased a pattern, wool scraps, and a cutter. Tacking her pattern to an empty picture frame, she followed instructions in Charlotte Stratton's 1955 book *Rug Hooking Made Easy* and the rest is history.

Having studied with the best teachers rug hooking had to offer, Martha mastered fine shading but preferred the freedom and color of hooking primitive-style rugs.

A hundred plus rugs later, she and her husband live in Gainesville, Georgia. Here, pictured in chronological order are some of the rugs she hooked.

In 1968 while living in Connecticut, Martha Morris learned how to hook rugs by following written instruction. She soon found a teacher who taught her to make beautifully shaded rugs hooked with #3 (3/32") cut strips of woolen fabric. "Fruit and Leaves" is the first rug she made under the direction of Connie Charleson. Pattern maker unknown. Hooked by Martha Morris. Georgia. 1969. 30" x 44". *Courtesy of Martha A. Morris*.

"Caswell Fruit Runner" recalls early American theorem paintings of the first half of the 19th century. Designed by Edith Dana. Hooked by Martha Morris. Georgia. 1970. 28" x 69". *Courtesy of Martha A. Morris.*

Corner nosegays and leafy vines contain "Antique Flowers" by the dozen. Pattern maker unknown. Hooked by Martha Morris. Georgia. 1972. 36" x 53". *Courtesy of Martha A. Morris.*

Tiny elephants join the maze of creatures dwelling in "Farm and Forest Primitive." W. Cushing and Company pattern. Hooked by Martha Morris. Georgia. 1975. 23" x 36". *Courtesy of Martha A. Morris.*

Rich shades of green used for foliage and field complement "Grandmother's Flower Garden." An inward facing clamshell border frames the reverse image floral display. Pattern maker unknown. Hooked by Martha Morris. Georgia. 1975. 48" x 27". *Courtesy of Martha A. Morris.*

A smiling whale tosses the occupant of an air borne dory as sailors row by. With her hook and strips of wool, Martha Morris hooked a modern reproduction of a mid-19th century rug. Lib Callaway pattern. Hooked by Martha Morris. Georgia. 1976. 25" x40". *Courtesy of Martha A. Morris.*

Floral sprays, complete with bleeding heart stems, protect a nest with two eggs. The proud cardinal father, of plaid hooked wings and tail, surveys the scene. "Bird and Nest." Lib Callaway patterns. Hooked by Martha Morris. Georgia. 1976. 30" x 44". *Courtesy of Martha A. Morris.*

Framed with a harmonizing diamond design edging, this still life "Fruit Basket" was hooked with a pleasing pastel palette. Lib Callaway patterns. Hooked by Martha Morris. Georgia. 1976. 25" x 34". *Courtesy of Martha A. Morris.*

A rug that's hooked with green, white and orange – the colors of the Irish flag – is bound to bring you luck. Mother cats and their kittens join shamrocks and primitive posies. Pattern maker unknown. Hooked by Martha Morris. Georgia. 1977. 26" x 53". *Courtesy of Martha A. Morris.*

Inspired by a 19th century embroidered floor covering found in the collection of New York's Metropolitan Museum of Art, Martha Morris hooked her own version of the "Caswell Carpet." A background of antique black enhances decorative fruit and flower motifs. Designed by Edith Dana. Hooked by Martha Morris. Georgia. 1977. 44" x 70". *Courtesy of Martha A. Morris.*

Framed by a plaid hooked shore, this lone "Fish" swims in curlicue waves on a scalloped sea. Lib Callaway patterns. Hooked by Martha Morris. Georgia. 1981. 30" x 42". *Courtesy of Martha A. Morris.*

Recalling posed Victorian portraitures, this hooked puppy is preserved for posterity. Designed by Edith Dana. Hooked by Martha Morris. Georgia. 1987. 30″ x 41″. *Courtesy of Martha A. Morris.*

Decorative concentric borders, including the little niceties of life, frame the "Village Horse." The central scene, complete with a rainbow, is child-like in its composition. Pattern Maker unknown. Hooked by Martha Morris. Georgia. 1990. 36″ x 44″. *Courtesy of Martha A. Morris.*

A hooked king of beast at rest in a bed of tulips – Martha-style. Deviating from the original design, "I changed the lion's face, added flowers and changed the finished shape from oval to rectangle." "The Lion." DiFranza Designs. Hooked by Martha Morris. Georgia. 1993. 41″ x 51″. *Courtesy of Martha A. Morris.*

A bit of hooked history. Under a full moon, "The Patriot," makes his memorable ride. Longfellow's famous words spur the rider on. Lib Callaway patterns. Hooked by Martha Morris. Georgia. 1994. 32" x 46". *Courtesy of Martha A. Morris.*

Changing from gold to green, billowing sunset clouds provide a dramatic setting for this hooked schooner under sail. Stylized wave motifs frame "Over the Bounding Main." Patsy Becker Designs. Hooked by Martha Morris. Georgia. 1996. 30" x 40". *Courtesy of Martha A. Morris.*

The "Sassafras Tree," covered in tweed and plaid bark, sprouts three different kinds of leaves and is the playground for birds, squirrels, a raccoon and bunny. Echoing some of the tree colors, a brick-like border was added to the pattern. Lib Callaway patterns. Hooked by Martha Morris. 1996. 60" x 40". *Courtesy of Martha A. Morris.*

Set on a black background, "Floral Antique" offers a colorful array of folk art flowers confined within a double clamshell border. Designed by Stella Hay Rex. Hooked by Martha Morris. Georgia. 1997. 41" x 70". *Courtesy of Martha A. Morris*.

With a full basket under her wing this hooked hen heads for home. As an adopted Georgian, Martha Morris made changes to the rug's original design. She added "Welcome Home" and a Confederate flag. At times controversial, the Confederate flag is considered a proud emblem of Southern heritage. Lib Callaway patterns. Hooked by Martha Morris. 1997. 26" x 36". *Courtesy of Martha A. Morris.*

"It Wonders Me," inspired by a Pennsylvania Dutch plate, gives praise for a bountiful harvest. Designed by Edith Dana. Hooked by Martha Morris. Georgia. 1998. 44" x 44". *Courtesy of Martha A. Morris.*

Preferring the "freedom and color of primitive rugs" it took Martha Morris thirty years to finish this finely shaded and detailed hooked floral study. "Garden's Gift." Designed by Pearl McGown. Hooked by Martha Morris. Georgia. 1969-1999. 46" x 29". Courtesy of *Martha A. Morris.*

"Caswell Carpet Squares" is a smaller and simplified version of the "Caswell Carpet" Martha Morris hooked in 1977. Pattern maker unknown. Hooked by Martha Morris. Georgia. 2000. 35" x 51". *Courtesy of Martha A. Morris.*

Hooking a remembrance of a very special day, Martha Morris's "Wedding Rug" honors a lifetime of love and devotion. Designed by Edith Dana. Hooked by Martha Morris. Georgia. 2001. 28" x 40". *Courtesy of Martha A. Morris.*

Showing her patriotic pride, Martha Morris hooked "United We Stand." Oak leaf branches frame a keen eyed eagle of impressive wingspan. Lib Callaway patterns. Hooked by Martha Morris. Georgia. 2003. 33" x 55". *Courtesy of Martha A. Morris.*

Holding hands and waving flags, two children lead the way to the "Quilt Shop." Solids, tweeds, plaids, and hand-dyed wools were used to hook this village scene of yesteryear. Pattern maker unknown. Hooked by Martha Morris. Georgia. 2004. 40" x 24". *Courtesy of Martha A. Morris.*

Re-visiting the past. Folks scurry about the village common on "Meeting Day." Note the fine shading and realistic details of the flag and meetinghouse door. Pattern maker unknown. Hooked by Martha Morris. Georgia. 2004. 39" x 50". *Courtesy of Martha A. Morris.*

Becky Jackson

A yard full of flowers was the inspiration behind "Mae-Time." Named for a hooking teacher and long time associate of Pearl McGown, this pattern offers fifteen different flowers, including gardenia and chrysanthemum. "I was introduced to hooking by a neighbor in the mid 80s. Work and other priorities took me away until 2006. Back attending classes with my friend, I have become 'hooked' and have been enjoying this fiber art." Designed by Jane McGown Flynn. House of Price / Charco pattern. Hooked by Becky Jackson. Georgia. 2008. 25.5" x 41". Courtesy of Becky Jackson.

LINDA BELL
Hiawassee, Georgia

Linda Bell has been hooking since 1980. "When I taught my left-handed ten-year old daughter to hook I decided I could be a teacher." And so she did. Receiving her McGown certification Linda has been teaching since 1986. She conducts weekly classes at her studio, teaches at rug camps and attends Teachers' Workshops. What follows is a sampling of her work.

"My 'Scraps' pillow was a teacher's project taught by Pat Gaufillet. This pattern had intrigued me for many years, so I was happy to have the chance to hook it." Designed by Jane McGown Flynn. House of Price / Charco pattern. Hooked by Linda Bell. Georgia. 2007. 16" x 16". *Courtesy of Linda Bell.*

"I was awarded a traveling scholarship to the McGown Western Teachers' Workshop in Eugene, Oregon. 'Old Time Oval' was one of the projects I started during that week in June 2007." Primco pattern by Della Griffiths. Hooked by Linda Bell. Georgia. 2007. 24" x 36.5". *Courtesy of Linda Bell.*

"Jasmine was my favorite 'grand-dog.' I fell in love with her on the day my son brought her home. My husband and I were her grandparents, her dog sitters, and her friends. I just had to hook her." Sadly Jasmine died in 2008 and "the hooked version has gone to live with her human family." Adapted from a photograph. Hooked by Linda Bell. Georgia. 2004. 17" x 19". *Courtesy of Linda Bell.*

"Hot Air Balloon." "I am part of a small hooking group who challenge ourselves to 'stretch' our hooking knowledge. We dyed the split-primary color wheel, and then had to use the wool we dyed in an original design." Designed and hooked by Linda Bell. Georgia. 2006. 14" x 10". *Courtesy of Linda Bell.*

"'Marie' was a teaching assignment for Teachers' Workshop. I was to teach trainees how to do fine shading on a rose. Not an easy task!" Designed by Jane McGown Flynn. House of Price / Charco pattern. Hooked by Linda Bell. Georgia. 2007. 15" x 15". *Courtesy of Linda Bell.*

"A 'Giraffe' has such an interesting face. Seeing one makes me smile." Adapted with permission from a *Zoobooks* cover image. Hooked by Linda Bell. Georgia. 2007. 20" x 16". *Courtesy of Linda Bell.*

"'Stained Glass Mosaic' was my first teaching assignment at Teachers' Workshop. I used only two of Bea Christoff's Transcolor formulas to complete the design elements of the pattern. I added spot dyes for the lead and the background. I was pleased with the result and with the simplicity of the color." Designed by Jane McGown Flynn. House of Price / Charco pattern. Hooked by Linda Bell. Georgia. 1987. 16" x 16". *Courtesy of Linda Bell.*

Painting with wool strips; an exquisitely shaded and hooked "Iris O'Keeffe." Designed by Jane McGown Flynn. House of Price / Charco pattern. Hooked by Linda Bell. Georgia. 1992. 13" x 13". *Courtesy of Linda Bell.*

Another hooked work of art; "Magnolia." Designed by Jane McGown Flynn. House of Price / Charco pattern. Hooked by Linda Bell. Georgia. 1988. 13" x 13". *Courtesy of Linda Bell.*

"As a challenge, our hooking group used black dye from four different manufacturers to see what the differences would be. We each designed an Oriental-style rug and hooked with the wools we dyed." "Grey Scale Color Journey." Designed and hooked by Linda Bell. Georgia. 2008. 12" x 18". *Courtesy of Linda Bell.*

PEARSON PARKER DESIGNS
Thomasville, Georgia

"I have been designing for national companies for years and needed a break. I walked into our library and the Wiregrass rug hooking group invited me to join them. I had hooked a rug several years ago and fell in love with it all over again."

Michelle Westberg now designs hooked rug patterns: fresh, fun and hand-drawn on fine linen. Available through Pearson Parker Designs.

Michelle Westberg

Detail of "Sweet Caroline." *Courtesy of M. Westberg*.

"Sweet Caroline" was inspired by the impending arrival of a first grandchild. Designed and hooked by Michelle Westberg. Georgia. 2008. 36" x 53". *Courtesy of M. Westberg.*

CLOSING

In closing it is my sincere wish that this author, straight from the Heart of New England, has represented the rug hookers of The Deep South in a manner that will not only make you proud but will make the rest of the country (and the world) sit up and take notice. I have experienced true Southern hospitality and I sincerely thank you.